T0370348

THE WAY
OF THE
Grateful
HEART

*Encountering Life
with Prayers of Praise*

SUSAN BROWN

WESTBOW
PRESS®
A DIVISION OF THOMAS NELSON
& ZONDERVAN

WestBow Press books may be ordered through booksellers or by contacting:

WestBow Press
A Division of Thomas Nelson & Zondervan
1663 Liberty Drive
Bloomington, IN 47403
www.westbowpress.com
844-714-3454

ISBN: 979-8-3850-1542-9 (sc)
ISBN: 979-8-3850-1552-8 (hc)
ISBN: 979-8-3850-1553-5 (e)

Library of Congress Control Number: 2023924429

Print information available on the last page.

WestBow Press rev. date: 08/27/2024

Contents

Background and a Word of Explanation

This book offers prayers of praise to God. It's about gratitude not only for what the Almighty has done for us, but about who he is: his character, his promises, and his desire for us to see beyond ourselves into the stunning beauty of his Presence.

Shifting our focus from the turbulence around us to the praise of the One with all power, knowledge, and wisdom can be life-altering. It is a gift of transformation from self-focus to worship.

God welcomes us to view our world in the proper perspective: under his watchful care, under his holy requirements, and under his justice and mercy. Soaking our minds and hearts in the knowledge of God as he is revealed in scripture refreshes and renews our spirit—a God-gift. We praise God because he is worthy of our time, our adoration, and our life commitment.

While praising God in depth and echoing scripture in gratitude, my ministry partners and I have experienced remarkable things. As we have praised and worshipped him around apartment complexes, churches, schools, prisons, and our homes, we have witnessed calm overtake conflict and peace replace worry. We have been blessed with courage and understanding beyond our ability. We have seen minds change, threats melt away, and danger averted. We have seen and felt evil flee. And always, we have known the blessing of unspeakable joy.

There are no petitions included in the following prayers. Certainly, we are welcome to ask for divine intervention. Our Father knows our needs before we ask, and we should pour out our hearts to him and run to him for help. But prayers of gratitude jolt our spirit into the truth that he is God, and he is with us. He is able and *is* intervening on our behalf. We know we are held in his hands.

Praise is personal.

Just as Jesus praised God as "Father" in the Lord's Prayer (Model Prayer, Matthew 6:9–13), these prayers of praise address God in terms of his relationship to us such as Ever-Present God and God Who Sees Me. Some may debate whether we should pray to our Father, to Jesus Christ, or to the Holy Spirit. My answer is yes—in my experience, all are appropriate. Since God is one being, praise for the work of the Father, Son, and Holy Spirit flows naturally into one unified prayer in this book, but there are also praises specific to the work of Jesus who invites us to pray in his name—and always for the Father's will (see also John 14:13–14 and 16:23–26).

Why pray "in the name of Jesus"?

Scripture clearly states that we must come to God through Jesus. *"Jesus answered, 'I am the way and the truth and the life. No one comes to the Father except through me'"* (John 14:6). Jesus instructed his followers to pray in his name after his death and resurrection. *"In that day you will ask in my name. I am not saying that I will ask the Father on your behalf. No, the Father himself loves you because you have loved me and have believed that I came from God"* (John 16:26–27).

Why include topics for each prayer of praise?

Many recurring themes in the Bible find themselves woven into my own prayers of praise. These are a few. Rather than broad praises, I have found that concentrating my thoughts on specific attributes and issues leads me to more fully explore and embrace God's being and work. I am continually amazed at the answers and intervention revealed in his character.

A word about Bible translations

While there are many good translations of the Bible, most of the scripture verses in this work are quoted from the New International Version, the most widely sold contemporary English translation. It is important to say that there is more than one NIV translation of the Bible. Most scripture quoted here is from the 2011 text revision with slightly different English word choices than those found in the 1978 version. The revision is due to an ongoing dedication to biblical scholarship and commitment to translate the original wording into English that most closely matches contemporary speech in order to promote our understanding of the original text. (See https://www. christianbook.com/page/bibles/about-bibles/about-translations/ about-the-niv?event=Bibles|1001852.) The following translations are also used.

ERV	Easy-to-Read Version
ESV	English Standard Version
KJV	King James Version
NKJV	New King James Version
NLT	New Living Translation
TLB	The Living Bible

Through these prayers, you're invited to meditate with me on God's uniquely perfect, powerful character. You are invited to explore the heart-filling relationship between our Creator-Savior and the humanity he cherishes. I pray this book meets you wherever you are in life and draws your attention to the breathtaking supremacy of God in awestruck worship and gratitude.

Acknowledgments

This work began as a collection of scripture that deeply touched me as I prepared Bible studies for our multihousing ministry. But actually, it began much earlier. From a young age, I have been struck by the power and joy of praising God. My brothers and I had a mother who knew—really knew—what it meant to follow Jesus. The joy of the Lord radiated from her, and she spoke peace into many hard situations. I am grateful for her love and steady, calm wisdom.

I'm also grateful for my mentors who have cultivated the practice of praise, especially ministry partners Becky Clausen and Becky Melancon whose devotion to the Lord and heartfelt praise have encouraged and upheld me through the years. I'm thankful for the wise words and steadfast example of mentor Bobby Germany, a God-sent encourager. I'm grateful for the many friends whose insight helped steer this work and for input on design and clarity from my nephew, Matt Morse. Your words mean more than you know.

And I'm thankful for my brothers, Steve and David Morse, gifted teachers whose faith inspires us all. Thank you for considering this work wisely and critically.

Introduction

"...for the place where you are standing is holy ground."
Exodus 3:5

Moses was doing an ordinary thing, tending his father-in-law's sheep in the wilderness, when he encountered the astonishing Presence of God—in a bush that was burning but not consumed. He recognized that he was standing on holy ground (Exodus 3:1–17).

A glimpse of the divine dimension changed everything: his perception, his direction, and his life purpose. As God revealed his name, *I Am Who I Am*, he also revealed his character.

As we commune with God's Presence in praise, we are awakened to a startling truth: *We* are standing on holy ground.

We are invited to *"Enter his gates with thanksgiving and his courts with praise"* (Psalm 100:4).

It is our destiny.

Ultimately, we who believe will join saints and angels praising God in heaven, with a sound as powerful as a massive waterfall or a wall-shaking thunderstorm (Hebrews 12:22–24; Revelation 19:6–8).

But we don't have to wait. Our part in that chorus begins now.

Part of the gift of being human is to share in the celebration of the divine Presence. As we praise God, we revel in his perfection and goodness. We embrace the growing recognition that we are not adrift, not alone, but grounded and anchored in him.

Praise expresses truth.

In creating us to glorify him, our Creator and Sustainer also conferred on us the *privilege* of praise—the awesome, eye-opening joy of worship (Psalm 147:1). To praise God acknowledges and bathes us in truth: not temporary, situational, or conditional "truth" but absolute, transcendent truth.

To know him is to adore him. He deserves to hear us say that he is valuable to us, that we are glad he is holy and good, and that we are grateful he is our life-giver and soul-rescuer.

And there is more. To praise God is to honor, appreciate, and *experience* his character. As we speak to him about his unrivaled power and love, we explore his relationship with us and remind ourselves what he has done throughout history—the world's history and our own. He is the same mercy-filled, miracle worker yesterday, today, and tomorrow. He chose us and deliberately drew us close. We are in this life together.

Praise is an offering.

"Through Jesus, therefore, let us continually offer to God a sacrifice of praise—the fruit of lips that openly profess his name."
Hebrews 13:15

Genuine praise cannot be forced but bubbles up from the grateful recesses of the heart—the work of the Holy Spirit. So, as we offer praise to God, we experience intense fellowship that blesses both the giver and the receiver.

We are significant in God's eyes; time with him is treasured (Revelation 5:8). He has set his heart on us. He has created us with an eternal plan for sharing our mutual interests and a unique capacity for enjoying his closeness. Created in his image, only humans can offer to God what he perfectly offers us: real, reciprocal, wholehearted love. *"We love because he first loved us"* (1 John 4:19).

As we offer praise, we offer *ourselves* to God. We offer a gift of love, trust, and surrender that becomes an all-consuming ability to *"'Love the Lord your God with all your heart and with all your soul and with all your mind and with all your strength'"* (Mark 12:30).

Cultivating a habit of praise involves a sacrifice of time and concentration. It is deliberately laying down mental and emotional distractions in favor of meditation, however brief or lengthy, on our Creator's excellence. It shifts our focus from the fallen world to the foundation of our faith—the costly sacrifice of Christ to bring us to himself.

Absorbing the knowledge of his absolute power, perfect wisdom, and lavish love leads naturally to an impulse to praise him. We react spontaneously to the thrill of his creation, care, and intervention.

Praise is not contingent upon our circumstances.

This sacred communion is not a formula for convincing the Almighty to grant our wishes. His plans and power will always outweigh our (even wholesome) desires.

It *is* about the ultimate blessing: to honor and welcome his Presence always…

> **When we are rejoicing***: "Let them give thanks to the Lord for his unfailing love and his wonderful deeds for mankind. Let them sacrifice thank offerings and tell of his works with songs of joy"* (Psalm 107:21–22).

When we are in distress or afraid: *"Do not be anxious about anything, but in every situation, by prayer and petition, with thanksgiving, present your requests to God. And the peace of God, which transcends all understanding, will guard your hearts and your minds in Christ Jesus"* (Philippians 4:6).

When we are waiting for answers: *"We wait in hope for the LORD; he is our help and our shield. In him our hearts rejoice, for we trust in his holy name"* (Psalm 33:20–21).

Through ordinary and extraordinary days, praising God often has the side-effect of increasing discernment, changing our outlook, and erasing a sense of distance from God.

In a mindset of gratitude, we experience life with confidence in the power and attentiveness of the One who is for us (Romans 8:31–39), will never forsake us (Deuteronomy 31:8), whose thoughts and actions are higher (Isaiah 55:9), and whose grasp of us and our situation is complete (Psalm 147:5).

Acknowledging his Presence and character alters our attitudes. It becomes a proactive instrument for tackling formidable situations with anticipation, not fear.

It changes our responses to events.

It rewrites our emotional habits.

As we praise God, we become more aware of his transforming care and embrace the promised work of the Holy Spirit.

"But the fruit of the Spirit is love, joy, peace, forbearance, kindness, goodness, faithfulness, gentleness and self-control. Against such things there is no law."
Galatians 5:22–23

Praise reveals and welcomes God's power over spiritual opposition.

"I pray that the eyes of your heart may be enlightened in order that you may know the hope to which he has called you, the riches of his glorious inheritance in his holy people, and his incomparably great power for us who believe. That power is the same as the mighty strength he exerted when he raised Christ from the dead and seated him at his right hand in the heavenly realms."
Ephesians 1:18-20

In the cosmic clash between good and evil, God, through Jesus, has already won. Believers in Christ are rescued from Satan's rule and transferred to his kingdom. As we see events unfold, acknowledging this truth brings understanding. Praise inspires hope. It unveils power.

Praising God can even change the atmosphere.

Filling our homes, workspaces, and communities with praise is powerful. Praising him room by room, desk by desk, or street by street brings insight, reveals his compassion, builds confidence, and embraces his power. As we fill our space with praise, understanding filters down into our minds and hearts—driving out pessimism and the paralysis of hopelessness and replacing them with the light of God's presence.

Praise also reminds the enemy of our souls that God rules. His sovereignty is undeniable, and he cares deeply for his human creation and the world he formed. A focus on evil can consume our thoughts and give Satan the attention he desires. We don't overcome evil by studying it or continually dwelling on the details of our hurt. Praising God places the spotlight where it belongs: on the power, love, and activity of God and the complete authority of Jesus Christ.

God is present, he sees it all, he is able, and he is good—even when that long-sought blessing seems elusive. The psalmists often came before God not only with hearts full of praise and gratitude, but also with grief, anxiety, and weariness from illness or opposition. And yet, they wrapped their petitions in abundant praise and confidence that while trouble is fleeting—even issues of life and death—God is forever trustworthy. He is forever praiseworthy.

Praise is an act of faith.

Praise is powerful because it is a statement of faith. And God both inspires and honors faith. It is his choice; it is his blessing to draw us into his Presence in faith and praise as he works seen and unseen on our behalf.

Scripture records many examples of God's work to motivate expressions of honor and gratitude *before and after* he displays his power.

Moses' face glowed after spending time in the Presence of God (Exodus 34:29). Worshipping and confessing the sins of his people, he received a covenant and a promise to do wonders: *"The people you live among will see how awesome is the work that I, the LORD, will do for you"* (Exodus 34:10). He saw opposition melt away, hearts change, bodies heal, needs abundantly met, and prayers answered for his wayward family and community.

When Solomon dedicated the temple, countless people sang praise to God for his goodness and faithful love. As the Ark of the Covenant was brought into the temple, God's Presence took over the building, and they stood in awe: *"Then the temple of the LORD was filled with the cloud, and the priests could not perform their service because of the cloud, for the glory of the LORD filled the temple of God"* (2 Chronicles 5:13–14).

King Jehoshaphat faced an overwhelming crisis by fasting and recognizing the intervening power of God. In faith, he prayed, *"For we have no power to face this vast army that is attacking us. We do not know what to do, but our eyes are on you"* (2 Chronicles 20:12). As people sang and praised God ahead of the army, their enemies attacked and destroyed each other. *"Do not be afraid or discouraged because of this vast army. For the battle is not yours, but God's"* (2 Chronicles 20:15).

Faced with persecution, the apostles Peter and John were ordered to stop speaking in the name of Jesus. Believers responded by praising God for his sovereignty and acknowledging the miracle-working authority of Jesus. *"After they prayed, the place where they were meeting was shaken. And they were all filled with the Holy Spirit and spoke the word of God boldly"* (Acts 4:31).

God's power has not diminished over time; his love remains relentless. His purposes prevail. And we are part of his plan.

We have been given a Spirit of *"power, love, and self-discipline"* (2 Timothy 1:7). We can *"approach God's throne of grace with confidence, so that we may receive mercy and find grace to help us in our time of need"*—to stand firm and to resist temptation (Hebrews 4:16).

As God reveals who he was, and is, and will forever be, he gives us a mind to understand and a heart to follow. We can sincerely pray, as Jesus prayed, to accomplish God's will, *"for it is God who works in you to will and to act in order to fulfill his good purpose"* (Philippians 2:13).

This is not an improbable scenario; this is our future. This is the way we are to live life. Once we get a sense of the gift that is ours—his goodness, his power, his direction, and his heartfelt care—praise echoes through our days, and our souls soar.

Making the Most of this Book

This book is designed to encourage a habit of praise: a lifestyle of gratitude to God. The praises written here come from many years of walking with the Lord. So, don't be surprised if prayers of praise don't come naturally or easily at first.

As you read each day's thoughts, ask God to help you praise him from your heart. Don't rush. Take time to think. Highlight the thoughts that stand out. You might want to write a word, thought, or Bible verse and place it where you can see it throughout the day—in your workspace or your pocket.

Make it personal.

As you read, examine who God is in light of your own experience. Add your praises and bring your concerns to him. Write your thoughts in the margins. Consider making a note when God answers prayers—your own personal record of his faithfulness.

What if I don't feel like it…

Sometimes, you may not feel like praising God on an issue. Don't give up! Pray for him to reveal his work in you and for you. Pray for understanding. Save the spot and reread it later. God knows the perfect time to apply the truth you need to hear.

If you can't read an entire prayer at once, don't be discouraged. It's okay to take your time and meditate on just one paragraph at a time. But keep going.

In every season of life there is a reason to praise God. *Every season.* Sometimes it's hard to focus on his goodness and easy to get stuck in anxiety. God welcomes us to bring our cares to him—those things that consume our thinking (Matthew 7:11). But when our prayers focus solely on our needs, we deny our souls the deeper communion and understanding available to those who meditate first and intentionally on God's character (Habakkuk 3:17-20). We need to "preach to ourselves" about his unfailing love and power.

Most importantly, God is worthy of our praise. He values our efforts to explore his character in worship. He also values our questions. A genuine search for truths about his attributes leads to deeper answers, and he has promised wisdom.

May this book refresh and redirect your thinking: God is able, loving, and on your side. Together, let's cultivate a habit of praise.

Abide

Whoever confesses that Jesus is the Son of God,
God abides in him, and he in God.
And we have known and believed
the love that God has for us.
1 John 4:15-16 (NKJV)

I will say to the LORD, "My refuge and my
fortress, my God, in whom I trust."
Psalm 91:2 (ESV)

Blessed are those who have learned to acclaim you,
who walk in the light of your presence, LORD.
They rejoice in your name all day long;
they celebrate your righteousness.
Psalm 89:15-16

God Who Walks with Me,

I worship you today as the One with absolute power and unrestrained love. Thank you teaching me to be ever-conscious of your Presence—not only to acknowledge your existence but to adore you.

I praise you for reminding me—this day—that time with you is a precious priority. Thank you for revealing that my purpose, my peace, and my deepest fulfillment come from your command: "Abide in Me, and I in you" (John 15:4 NKJV).

1

As I speak your name over the noise of this day, I am grateful to experience the stunning reality of your Presence: you are watching, intervening, and creating pathways beyond my ability. I praise you for a sense of soul-cleansing wellness, security, and wholeness. You are where I belong. You are my home.

Knowing that you are with me, and for me, I thank you for leading me today into soul-searching honesty and openness with you, the One who understands all things (Psalm 51:6). In the embrace of your Spirit, waywardness gives way to willing obedience, and your love, joy, and peace radiate through my being.

> Today, I thank you for calling me
> to do what I cannot do
> without your Spirit abiding in me.
>
> I am grateful for the blessing of a life
> united with you as your Spirit *in* me
> flows naturally *through* me today
> to transform my heart and my surroundings
> with your kindness and peace.

In Jesus' name I pray and praise you, amen.

Always

My Ever-Present God,

I am so grateful to be constantly within your sight, permanently anchored in you, and sincerely welcomed by you, the One who holds the universe by the force of your word. As you hover over humanity and inhabit my heart, nothing escapes your attention. *In this moment, in this circumstance, you are here, surrounding and filling me with your Presence.*

Thank you, Lord Jesus, for enduring the cross for the joy of seeing us in harmony (Hebrews 12:2). *This was always your plan*: to transfer me from the kingdom of darkness into your kingdom of light. I praise you for your loving insight—for revealing my self-deception and casual attitude toward sin's death spiral.

Your commitment never ends (Lamentations 3:22–23). Whenever sin and shame seek to blind me to the warmth and power of your Presence, I am grateful to know that you are still with me as I look to you (James 4:8).

As I absorb this precious gift, I praise you for drawing me into faithfulness so that turning to you throughout the day becomes as natural as breathing. As I intentionally look to you in all things, your truth filters through my thoughts and I begin to comprehend how tenderly—and purposefully—you are watching and nurturing me today.

Thank you for calling me to offer myself as a "living sacrifice" and reminding me that you steadfastly work in me to produce the will and ability to speak and act in your name (Romans 12:1; Philippians 2:13). How reassuring it is to know that you are always trustworthy, even when my confidence or obedience falters.

As I am attentive to you today, I am grateful to see
your power and peace pour through my life
to encourage those around me
and point their gaze toward you,
my true Companion and the love of my life.

In the name of Jesus, I pray. Amen.

Almighty

*"Holy, holy, holy is the Lord God Almighty,
who was, and is, and is to come."*
Revelation 4:8

*Who is like you, Lord God Almighty? You, Lord, are
mighty, and your faithfulness surrounds you.*
Psalm 89:8

*Acknowledge that the Lord is God! He made us, and we
are his. We are his people, the sheep of his pasture.*
Psalm 100:3 (NLT)

God Who Watches Over Me,

How breathtaking it is to be welcomed into your Presence—to know that your love and strength surround me, and your hand directs my life. I am secure in the knowledge that you are God, and I am yours. Thank you for reminding me today that you are, in reality, all-powerful and perfect.

- ❅ I praise you as the Source and Author of Life. In a deliberate act of love, you created humanity in your image, and you sustain all things (Genesis 1:1, 26–28; Hebrews 1:3).
- ❅ You are the Holy One. You are worthy of my complete trust (Psalm 33:21; Romans 15:13).
- ❅ You are the Just One. You guide me into right thinking and intervene on behalf of justice now, and you will bring ultimate justice on earth (Jeremiah 9:24).

❋ You are my Defender: You are my Safe Place and Wise Advocate (Hebrews 6:19-20; John 14:23).

Lord Jesus, I honor you for your authority over every form of evil. Thank you for valuing me enough to pay the penalty on the cross for my own selfish vices. I praise you for drawing me into holiness even when I stubbornly discarded your transforming power as impossible or undesirable.

I am so grateful that I can count on you to win the spiritual battles reflected in my earthly struggles, knowing that "the one who is in you is greater than the one who is in the world" (1 John 4:4). Thank you for teaching me to view myself as you see me: as a conqueror, as salt that seasons the world with wisdom, and as one who carries light and hope.

> Almighty One, nothing is beyond your ability,
> and everything is within your gaze.
> As you hold me in your arms,
> I thank you for peace beyond my understanding,
> power that overwhelms,
> and love that saturates my soul.
>
> In the name of Jesus, I pray. Amen.

Answer

"Call to me and I will answer you and tell you great
and unsearchable things you do not know."
Jeremiah 33:3

You answer us with awesome and righteous deeds, God our Savior,
the hope of all the ends of the earth and of the farthest seas.
Psalm 65:5

I will praise the Lord, who counsels me;
even at night my heart instructs me.
I keep my eyes always on the Lord.
Psalm 16:7-8

All-Knowing God,

You are God of the whole earth, the Designer of my mind, the God who sees me. I praise you for the stunning revelation of your love and wisdom. You are more than a vague, unknowable force; you are a living Being. You are not distant; you are a vibrant Presence within me.

Only you perfectly perceive all things with a view of eternity. Thank you for *inviting* me to seek your insight, direction, and intervention. Thank you for faith that you will answer because you are good, you have promised, and you are mine.

I praise you because your answers are more profound and compassionate than I have imagined. Thank you for trust to accept your answers and your timing even when I must wait and weep (John 11:40–44) or when I cannot see the good you are accomplishing (Isaiah 55:9).

When my heart cries out for hope, I thank you for reminding me that you are my Living Hope. Thank you for showing me that understanding *why* is not as instructive or comforting as learning to lean on you.

Thank you for continuing to answer the heartfelt prayers of those who came before me and for the knowledge that my present prayers will reverberate through time as you work out all things according to your purposes.

As you see into the future
you have prepared for me,
I thank you for teaching me
to seek you first
and rely on you always,
my Perfect Advisor and Faithful Friend.

In the name of Jesus, I pray. Amen.

Anxiety

*When I said, "My foot is slipping," your unfailing
love, LORD, supported me. When anxiety was great
within me, your consolation brought me joy.*
Psalm 94:18–19

*Do not be anxious about anything, but in every situation, by
prayer and petition, with thanksgiving, present your requests to
God. And the peace of God, which transcends all understanding,
will guard your hearts and your minds in Christ Jesus.*
Philippians 4:6–7

God my Keeper,

I praise you today for your power over anxious thoughts. You are the
Prince of Peace: knowing that you are in control of my life brings
assurance that you will guard, guide, and nourish my soul with
the awareness of your never-ending love. I am unceasingly in your
hands.

Thank you for filling my mind with the truth that I am secure in your
family and always in your thoughts. As waves of soul healing wash
through me, I praise you for your unending compassion, patience,
and perseverance on my behalf.

You are the Source that illuminates my way and the water that
satisfies my thirsty soul. In days of celebration, moments of stress,
and seasons of instability, *you* are here. As I seek your company,

your uplifting Presence sooths, steadies, and speaks wisdom—and inevitably the foundation of joy returns.

I am so glad that you are *constantly* working out your purposes for me. My Wonderful Counselor, in your perfect knowledge, you understand that circumstances and emotions will attempt to overtake my thinking. Thank you for making it clear that you are always available and infallible: you have overcome the world (John 16:33).

Thank you for reminding me that you alone are my sacred stability, my contentment, and my resting place. Thank you for calling me to meditate on things that are good and praiseworthy (Philippians 4:8).

As you fill my thoughts with your Presence,
stress and sorrow fade
into a celebration of who you are,
and I gratefully relax and release
my life into your care,
my nourishing, life-giving
Good Shepherd.
I am eternally grateful.

In the name of Jesus, I pray. Amen.

Battle

God my Defender,

I honor you today as the Lord of Heaven's Armies, the Holy Conquering One, and my Protector. You have all authority and complete knowledge of the upheavals I face—even before they occur. As I soak in the reality of your mercy and power, you are already at work to bring order out of chaos and love out of loss. I thank you that I am *eternally secure* in your care.

Lord of the Universe, you are my foundation and my safe place. I praise you for keeping my eyes fixed firmly on you. Thank you for the assurance that you are always present, never shaken by events, and able to supply the right words, attitudes, and actions for everything that happens today.

Thank you for equipping me with a spirit of "power, love and self-discipline" (2 Timothy 1:7). Because you are the one who goes with me, watches over me, and fights for me, I will not panic, run, or ignore trouble but face the battle head-on. Thank you for your promise never to leave nor forsake me and to bring good out of all things for those who love you (Romans 8:28; Hebrews 13:5).

As I think through the conflicts and opportunities I face today, I praise you for preparing me with wisdom to plan and act. Thank you for teaching me to respond to evil with good and to ask for your intervention—not only for myself but also for those who oppose me.

Thank you for your command to treat others
as I want to be treated (Luke 6:31): to respect,
forgive, and offer advice in a spirit of kindness.
I am grateful to expect God-surprises as I pray
for blessings on difficult people (Matthew 5:44-45),
including the ultimate blessing—
a heart that worships you.

In the name of Jesus, I pray. Amen.

Become

But to all who believed him and accepted him,
he gave the right to become children of God.
John 1:12 (NLT)

Jesus answered, "Everyone who drinks this water will be
thirsty again, but whoever drinks the water I give them
will never thirst. Indeed, the water I give them will become
in them a spring of water welling up to eternal life."
John 4:13–14

God of All Knowledge,

I am in awe of you, the master designer and relentless builder. You see straight into my soul, knowing what I have been, what I am, and what I will become. As you move your people into our stunningly beautiful future, I praise you for placing me as a building block in the kingdom you mapped out before the creation of the world.

I praise you, Lord Jesus, as the "founder and perfecter of our faith" (Hebrews 12:2 ESV). Thank you for *becoming sin* for me, shouldering my wrongdoing, and taking my eternal consequence on yourself (2 Corinthians 5:21). In the prime of your life, you considered my soul precious enough to give up your future on earth for an eternity with me (John 14:1–3).

Father God, thank you for continuously shaping me so that I become a true, faithful reflection of Christ. Thank you for unfolding layer after layer of truth so that my words and the meditation of my heart become pleasing to you (Psalm 19:14).

My Guide and Teacher, your purposes stand forever. Thank you for reminding me that you are the good and flawless One: I must stand on your strength as I wait on your process. Thank you for the *gift* of waiting. It is a time for faith to deepen and experience in your Presence to grow—as I fully depend on you (2 Corinthians 4:7).

As I lean into you this day, I thank you for aligning my life with your plans and constructing a soul-satisfying and profoundly greater, richer life than I have imagined (Acts 4:11–12).

I am grateful to become
a permanent member of your family:
"God's special possession" (1 Peter 2:9).
Thank you for opportunities to become
a conduit of hope to those around me
so that your praise
echoes throughout this day.

In the name of Jesus, I pray. Amen.

Bitterness

*"And I will give you a new heart—I will give you new and
right desires—and put a new spirit within you. I will take out
your stony hearts of sin and give you new hearts of love."*
Ezekiel 36:26 (TLB)

*Get rid of all bitterness, rage and anger, brawling and slander,
along with every form of malice. Be kind and compassionate to one
another, forgiving each other, just as in Christ God forgave you.*
Ephesians 4:31–32

*He restores my soul;
He leads me in the paths of righteousness
For His name's sake.*
Psalm 23:3 (NKJV)

My Gracious God,

I praise you for seeing deeply into my wounded heart with
understanding and love. Thank you for replacing the joy-robbing
focus on disappointment and hurt with your love and peace.

You alone are perfectly merciful and gracious; you alone are
completely trustworthy and faithful. As I pour out my soul to you,
I thank you for the sacred invitation to examine my distress in your
Presence and release it into your care (1 Peter 5:7). I praise you—
from my heart—as the One whose soul-filling love is so powerful
and thorough that it washes away even the root of bitterness buried
at my core.

Thank you for enabling me to surrender any thoughts of revenge into your wise, almighty hands. Thank you for teaching me that although harm may occur—even devastating harm—I am called to be a peacemaker.

Thank you for transforming my mind to embrace your selfless definition of love—for teaching me to be kind and patient rather than easily angered. Thank you for specifically instructing your people to avoid spreading discord and to show that harmony and wholeness are possible by our godly example (James 3:18).

Thank you for teaching me not to dwell on the past but to perceive the new things you are doing. I praise you for allowing me to see my life through your eyes and recognize that *my sin* was buried with you—a costly, self-sacrificing gift—and I am raised to new life.

Thank you for forgiving me *completely*
and redirecting me to walk
in the beautiful freedom of forgiveness,
in your power, in your heart.

In the name of Jesus, I pray. Amen.

Boldness

In the day when I cried out,
You answered me,
And made me bold
with strength in my soul.
Psalm 138:3 (NKJV)

Let us therefore come boldly to the throne of grace, that we
may obtain mercy and find grace to help in time of need.
Hebrews 4:16 (NKJV)

After they prayed, the place where they were meeting
was shaken. And they were all filled with the Holy
Spirit and spoke the word of God boldly.
Acts 4:31

God My Commander,

Thank you for the freedom of utter confidence in you. I praise you as the One who knows all things and prepares the path ahead of me to accomplish your good purposes. "For the eyes of the LORD range throughout the earth to strengthen those whose hearts are fully committed to him" (2 Chronicles 16:9).

Thank you, Lord Jesus, for the courage, obedience, and love that drove you to self-sacrifice on my behalf. As I meditate on your life and work today, I thank you for keeping your eyes on the goal: to present me spotless, with great joy, to our Father (Jude 1:24).

❊ Lord Jesus, thank you for preparing yourself and arming me with **scripture** deeply entrenched in my mind so that I can perceive evil and reject temptation.

❊ I praise you for **praying** for us as you set your sights on the cross and for equipping me to boldly follow you.

❊ I honor you for **acting decisively**, even allowing your life on earth to be cruelly ended by those who didn't understand your divine mission. Thank you for motivating me to be intentional in prayer and to embrace the assignment to speak the truth in love.

I am simply overwhelmed by your authority and plans. Thank you for inviting me to bring my concerns and questions to you. And on those days when I feel inadequate, I am grateful to know that you enter my challenges with the power that created the world and the wisdom to achieve unimaginable, far-reaching results.

I praise you for sending me out boldly with the assurance
that you have overcome the world
and that I walk through this day *with you.*
Thank you for the privilege of sharing in your work—
and celebrating your victory.

In the name of Jesus, I pray. Amen.

Change

*Every good and perfect gift is from above, coming
down from the Father of the heavenly lights, who
does not change like shifting shadows.*
James 1:17

Jesus Christ is the same yesterday and today and forever.
Hebrews 13:8

*"Praise be to the name of God for ever and ever; wisdom
and power are his. He changes times and seasons;
he deposes kings and raises up others. He gives wisdom
to the wise and knowledge to the discerning."*
Daniel 2:20–21

My Constant God,

I am overflowing with gratitude as I focus on the many genuine, unchanging reasons to rejoice. Thank you for reminding me *today* that you are the One with all power, knowledge, and wisdom. *Today,* you are the One who treasures me, teaches me, and enjoys my company—and this will never change.

I honor you because you are ceaselessly good and tirelessly working. You know the end from the beginning, you clear the path, and you walk me through every life transition (Psalm 139:16).

When everything else changes—when people and situations don't live up to my expectations—you are my dependable, unchanging

One. Because you invite me to trust in you, I am not overwhelmed by events or people, but wrapped in your all-powerful arms (Psalm 55:22).

Thank you for teaching me to *expect* surprises—those that delight and those that dismay. How exhilarating it is to know you have prepared good work for me as a co-laborer with Christ *in these situations*. So, wherever you place me today, I am grateful for opportunities to demonstrate your steadiness and communicate your integrity in love as your Spirit leads.

Thank you for calling me to embrace you through the changes you bring, knowing that your paths have purpose, and your ways are best. Thank you for focusing my heart and my thoughts on you, recognizing that you are forever faithful and actively watching over me.

I praise you today for your unchanging love. Your compassion and ardent attention refresh me every day. As we experience peaks and valleys together, I thank you for inviting me to run to you and share the moments.

Consumed by your Presence and aware of your hand at work,
I am filled with praise—and anticipation.

Thank you. In the name of Jesus, I pray. Amen.

Confess

If we confess our sins, he is faithful and just and will forgive us our sins and purify us from all unrighteousness. If we claim we have not sinned, we make him out to be a liar and his word is not in us.
1 John 1:9–10

Do not remember the sins of my youth and my rebellious ways; according to your love remember me, for you, LORD, are good.
Psalm 25:7

My Holy, Restoring God,

I honor you as the One who knows me completely and invites me to follow you wholeheartedly into holiness. You are faithful, flawless, and fiercely opposed to sin that inevitably brings hurt and painful consequences to me, your cherished child.

Lord Jesus, thank you for reminding me today of the weight of sorrow, pain, and shame you shouldered for me on the cross to vindicate me of every charge that could be brought against me before Heaven (Romans 8:33-34). Thank you for confronting my unruly heart and mind with the knowledge of my sin: "But who can discern their own errors? Forgive my hidden faults" (Psalm 19:12).

All-Knowing God, I praise you for opening my mind to understand that confession to you—the One from whom nothing is hidden—brings deep soul wellness and renewing closeness (James 5:16; Psalm 32:1–11). Thank you for guiding me to confess not only to you but also to other people: bringing sin into the open robs it of its deceptive power and brings deep healing.

> *"Blessed is the one whose sin the LORD does not count*
> *against them and in whose spirit is no deceit."*
> Psalm 32:2

Thank you for reminding me today that your Light can even change the environment around me as your holiness takes over.

Thank you for always providing a way out of temptation by turning to you (1 Corinthians 10:13). I am so grateful to experience the goodness I receive from you as you lead me into sincere obedience and self-control (2 Timothy 1:7).

> I am amazed by this truth: Because you love me,
> you welcome me to come to you
> with a clean conscience, a fresh start,
> and a heart overflowing
> with genuine, grateful love.

> In the name of Jesus, I pray and praise you. Amen.

Consider

*Consider the ravens: They do not sow or reap, they
have no storeroom or barn; yet God feeds them. And
how much more valuable you are than birds!*
Luke 12:24

*I pray that the eyes of your heart may be enlightened in
order that you may know the hope to which he has called
you, the riches of his glorious inheritance in his holy people,
and his incomparably great power for us who believe.*
Ephesians 1:18–19

Almighty God,

I praise you today for making yourself *known*—for inviting me to
perceive the joy of existence through your eyes and in your Presence.
How firmly I am held; how deeply I am loved! You are my abundant
Provider, my Strength, and my Security.

Thank you for reminding me not to take your love and mercy lightly.
Thank you for revealing that your benevolence and your "no excuses"
stand against sin are both part of your excellent character—and
your expectation for me (Romans 1:18-20). As the One who daily
considers everything I do, I honor you for drawing me into a *life* of
faithfulness. In your relentless love, you continue to cut away things
that are not pleasing to you: things that wreck lives and wreak havoc
in your beloved world.

Lord Jesus, thank you for calling me to consider the intense temptation and opposition you faced on earth. Thank you for drawing me close during hard times so that my faith is not shattered but strengthened in the knowledge that you are with me. Thank you for teaching me that suffering produces a weightiness—a depth of faith—that is rarely achieved elsewhere (James 1:2).

As I lean into your Presence, I praise you for insight beyond my ability. Thank you for welcoming me to ask for wisdom and promising an abundant supply (James 1:5).

Thank you for teaching me to stop and consider your complete, compassionate care for me. Like your wildflowers, I also bloom under your attention because you have given me spiritual roots and living water.

> Today, I thank you for opening my soul
> to see your constant work,
> a mind to understand your awesome character,
> and a heart to appreciate you.

In the name of Jesus, I pray and praise you. Amen.

Decisions

I will instruct you and teach you in the way you should
go; I will counsel you with my loving eye on you.
Psalm 32:8

For this God is our God for ever and ever;
he will be our guide even to the end.
Psalm 48:14

"This, then, is how you should pray: 'Our Father in
heaven, hallowed be your name, your kingdom come,
your will be done, on earth as it is in heaven.'"
Matthew 6:9–10

All-Wise God,

I look to you as my Gracious Guide and Loving Counselor. You are the Source of all knowledge and the only One with perfect insight into the past, present, and future. As you have led your people throughout history, you also lead today. Thank you for walking ahead of me, guarding my back, and covering me with your Presence (Psalm 139:5). You know the plans you have for me (Jeremiah 29:11). So, as I lean into you, trusting in your goodness, I am grateful to pray for your will in every decision.

You are the ultimate authority: You hold both logical and emotional concerns in flawless balance. You are the Spirit of Truth; you alone fully comprehend my choices and all outcomes. I am so grateful to talk everything over in your holy Presence.

Lord Jesus, thank you for calling me to first align my life with yours so that I hear you in the ordinary moments as well as the crossroads or crises. Thank you for bringing to mind any disobedience to directions already revealed in your scripture: sin that clouds my judgment. Thank you for guiding me to see beyond current circumstances or the pressure of other people to embrace decisions that advance your kingdom:

- ✳ to honor God and not compromise or harm those around me (Matthew 22:37–39).
- ✳ to choose paths that bring peace and build up the faith and godliness of others (Romans 14:19).
- ✳ to surrender to your purposes—not try to squeeze you into my concept of success (Isaiah 55:9).

Thank you for unveiling your direction step-by-step,
so that I experience a blessing
profoundly higher than simply sound decisions:
the precious process of walking in your Presence,
focused on you.

Thank you. In the name of Jesus, I pray. Amen.

Delight

*For the Lord takes delight in his people; he crowns
the humble with victory. Let his faithful people rejoice
in this honor and sing for joy on their beds.*
Psalm 149:4–5

*"But let the one who boasts boast about this: that they
have the understanding to know me, that I am the Lord,
who exercises kindness, justice and righteousness on
earth, for in these I delight," declares the Lord.*
Jeremiah 9:24

God, My Delight,

Thank you for inviting me to live *with you*, to experience life together, sharing laughter and love, loss and restoration. In this moment, as I pause to reflect on you, your Spirit infuses the very atmosphere with peace and purpose. *Everything* is made better by your Presence.

I praise you for delighting in **compassion** that yields both powerful justice and tender mercy. Thank you for refusing to compromise on sin that distracts and wounds me. I honor you for shedding light on my misconceptions—even wrong thinking passed down through generations.

I delight in your **patience**. I am grateful for the way you draw me gently into understanding and never give up on me. In your desire to share the beautiful experience of holiness, you transform my heart, inspire my will, and welcome me back from every rebellious path (Psalm 51:10).

Thank you for your **love**. Knowing that you are fully faithful draws me increasingly into loving delight in you, and I soak in the knowledge that I am forever cherished.

Thank you for reminding me today of the depth of your care.

- ❋ You are pleased to rescue and adopt me—even at the cost of your blood. I belong to the family of God (Isaiah 53:10–12 NKJV; 1 Peter 1:18–19).
- ❋ You invite me to ask for your wisdom and intervention and gladly welcome this act of faith (1 Kings 3:9–10).
- ❋ You are delighted when I come to you in trusting prayer, surrendering to your higher judgment (Psalm 147:11; Isaiah 55:9).

As I take delight in your Presence,
I am so grateful to see the desires of my heart
match the desires of your heart (Psalm 37:4),
and I run to worship you, my Source of Joy.

In the name of Jesus, I pray. Amen.

Desire

You open your hand and satisfy the desires of every living thing.
Psalm 145:16

"As the rain and the snow come down from heaven,
and do not return to it without watering the earth
and making it bud and flourish, so that it yields seed for the
sower and bread for the eater, so is my word that goes out from
my mouth: It will not return to me empty, but will accomplish
what I desire and achieve the purpose for which I sent it."
Isaiah 55:10–11

Yes, Lord, walking in the way of your laws, we wait for you;
your name and renown are the desire of our hearts.
Isaiah 26:8

God Who Satisfies My Soul,

Your Presence—wrapped in righteousness, love, and peace—is desirable above all things. I praise you for steadily opening the eyes of my soul to comprehend this life-changing truth. My God Who Works Wonders, I am overwhelmed by your power and desire to remake my mind and heart so that my life-longings *actually* reflect your holiness.

Thank you for graciously providing the will to surrender my heart and mind to you today: to resist the temptation to ignore your sacred prompting or treat your precious Spirit carelessly. I am so grateful that you are not satisfied with casual compliance but invite me to honestly lay the conflicting desires of my heart at your feet.

As you probe the longings and coveted idols in the secret places of my mind, I praise you for leading me to abandon my self-focus and choose—really embrace—your purposes, no matter the cost. As I daily surrender my will in favor of your ways, I experience new depths of understanding and love in the abundant life you offer (Matthew 10:38).

Compassionate Lord, I praise you for revealing your greatest desire for me: to live united with you in love and purpose, intentionally looking to you in all things and shining the light of your kindness on your beloved humanity. Thank you for the unparalleled joy this stirs in my soul.

My Patient, Powerful God, thank you for giving me strength and anticipation as I walk into the future you desire for me.

Thank you for drawing me close so that I can
genuinely reflect and eagerly welcome your plans
as you unfold a future beyond my imagination
and produce a harvest of righteousness.

In the name of Jesus, I pray. Amen.

Devote

"For who is he who will devote himself to be close to me?" declares the LORD. "So you will be my people, and I will be your God."
Jeremiah 30:21–22

"No one can serve two masters. Either you will hate the one and love the other, or you will be devoted to the one and despise the other. You cannot serve both God and money."
Matthew 6:24

Now devote your heart and soul to seeking the Lord your God.
1 Chronicles 22:19

My Devoted God,

I am astounded by your commitment to me: you are loyal, attentive, and unwavering. As you view the entire expanse of time in intricate detail and loving perspective, I can trust that you are constantly working for the good of those who love you, including me. Thank you for reminding me today that your heart delights in providing generously for me from your world and from your Spirit. Thank you for revealing your favor in unexpected ways.

Your name thrills my soul. Thank you for calling me to devote myself to you, relinquishing my death grip on my own choices in favor of my real-life mission: to live infused with love for you and other people. As you draw me further into devotion, I am deeply grateful for the work of your Spirit.

✳ Thank you for reminding me that commitment is both inward and outward. Our mutual love comes with a commission—to be prepared to explain the life-changing hope I have in your Presence (1 Peter 3:15).

✳ I praise you for guiding me to the "way out" of temptation (1 Corinthians 10:13), knowing that the spiritual forces of evil will seek to undermine the faithful. Thank you for courage to reconcile differences and react with grace rather than grudges.

✳ I am so grateful for your free-flowing mercy and the motivation to spread kindness that is patient, encouraging, sacrificing, and ready to bless (1 Corinthians 13:4-6).

> Lord, thank you for inspiring the will
> to fully devote myself to you.
> I am grateful to be planted,
> nurtured, and flourishing in you,
> the One who "fills everything in every way"
> (Ephesians 1:22–23).

> In the name of Jesus, I pray. Amen.

Discipline

*My son, do not despise the LORD's discipline, and do
not resent his rebuke, because the LORD disciplines
those he loves, as a father the son he delights in.*
Proverbs 3:11–12

*No discipline seems pleasant at the time, but painful. Later on,
however, it produces a harvest of righteousness and peace.*
Hebrews 12:11

*Listen to advice and accept discipline, and at the
end you will be counted among the wise.*
Proverbs 19:20

All-Knowing God,

I praise you today as my Good Father: the One who is patient, kind, and tenaciously shaping me. Thank you for confronting my willful heart with flawlessly timed wisdom. I praise you for your deep compassion—for caring enough to invest your truth and time in lovingly disciplining me so that I may reflect your honor.

I am so grateful that no attitude or action is beyond your power or outside the reach of your love. Thank you for doing whatever it takes—even using circumstances and heartbreak—to get my attention and lovingly draw me to surrender to your righteousness.

I am so grateful that holiness is not an unrealistic or self-defeating quest, but a calling to come with you and walk the world together.

Thank you for showing me that—by your power—I can "throw off everything that hinders and the sin that so easily entangles" me (Hebrews 12:1).

Thank you for reminding me that you (not I) are the Great Judge, and you take seriously the sin of self-righteousness (Luke 6:37–38). Thank you for calling me to examine myself and yield to your discipline before critiquing or attempting to discipline the people around me (Matthew 7:3–5; Galatians 6:1–5).

Thank you for saturating your discipline with mercy
as you graciously reveal and remove
layer after layer of resistance.
I am forever grateful that you love me enough
to replace hardness with wholeness
and exchange sin for the lightness of living in real love,
permeating joy, and profound peace.

In the name of Jesus, I pray. Amen.

Encourage

*May our Lord Jesus Christ himself and God our
Father, who loved us and by his grace gave us eternal
encouragement and good hope, encourage your hearts
and strengthen you in every good deed and word.*
2 Thessalonians 2:16–17

*Finally, brothers and sisters, rejoice! Strive for full
restoration, encourage one another, be of one mind, live in
peace. And the God of love and peace will be with you.*
2 Corinthians 13:11

God Who Loves and Leads Me,

You are my Foundation, my Keeper, and the One who loves me unconditionally. How encouraging it is to know that you, the Creator and Overseer of the Universe, walk before me and surround me with favor like a shield (Psalm 5:12). This minute, this day, you are drawing me closer, working to train me, and strengthening my faith.

I am so grateful that I am intentionally created and valued by you. Thank you, Lord Jesus, that your concern and care for me are so deliberate—so extreme—that you even sacrificed yourself to exchange my sin for your holiness.

No matter how much I explore your love I cannot fully grasp it and will never see the end of it (Ephesians 3:18–19). I am so grateful that your hold on me is not based on my performance but on your kindness. Thank you for calling me to encourage those around me with this truth as I recount examples of your faithfulness (1 Thessalonians 5:10–11).

Thank you for assurance that I am yours, and your power and peace are always available to me as I look to you.

⁂ I am your child and your friend (John 1:12; John 15:15).
⁂ I belong to you (Romans 14:8).
⁂ I have direct access to you, anytime, through Jesus (Hebrews 4:16).
⁂ I am inspired and energized by your Spirit to do everything you call me to do (Philippians 2:13).

I am grateful today that you know every need before I speak of it, and you graciously invite me to talk it over, listen to you, and lean on you.

Thank you for *always* being with me
and ready to bless each day
with a fountain of wisdom and love
as I walk in the light of your Presence.

In the name of Jesus, I pray. Amen.

Endure

Your kingdom is an everlasting kingdom,
and your dominion endures
through all generations.
The LORD is trustworthy
in all he promises
and faithful in all he does.
Psalm 145:13

Give thanks to the LORD, for he is good; his love endures forever.
1 Chronicles 16:34

My Trustworthy, Timeless God,

Your word, your honor, and your love endure forever. Nothing—no adverse event, health issue, or challenging environment—can remove me from your hand. As I stand in your grace and rejoice in your goodness, I am consumed by peace. You are here.

I praise you, Lord Jesus, for your example of faithfulness in suffering. Thank you for your costly love and determination to bring me into your eternal family: *"Because of the joy awaiting him, he endured the cross"* (Hebrews 12:2 NLT). I am so grateful that I am never out of your powerful Presence. It is not up to me to find enough determination or stamina to make it, but you have given me your strength, your steadfastness, and your promise to guide every step and every decision.

On days when I am vigorous or seasons when I am fragile—when life seems under control or shifting unpredictably—you are my steadfast hope. Nothing is beyond the reach of your love and power, even the power to lay down your life and take it up again. So, I thank you for reminding me that you are always present: when I can't see your intervention, I can always trust your heart.

I am so grateful that you reveal and build my character when I must endure suffering. In physical or emotional pain, you bring unique insight and profound, precious closeness to you. I praise you for your patience—the way you draw me gently into understanding. Thank you for your deep, tender compassion and the revelation that I am truly cherished.

> My God, trusting you is like building my house
> *on solid rock* (Matthew 7:24-27).
> When the floods of change or crisis come,
> I am grateful to find my security, my hope,
> and my assurance in your everlasting arms.

> In the name of Jesus, I praise and pray. Amen.

Enemies

The LORD is my rock, my fortress and my deliverer; my God is my rock, in whom I take refuge, my shield and the horn of my salvation, my stronghold. I called to the LORD, who is worthy of praise, and I have been saved from my enemies.
Psalm 18:1–3

What, then, shall we say in response to these things? If God is for us, who can be against us? He who did not spare his own Son, but gave him up for us all—how will he not also, along with him, graciously give us all things?
Romans 8:31–32

All-Powerful God,

I am grateful today that you are my Refuge: your unfailing arms are a safe and welcoming place as I stand in the heat of opposition. Thank you for covering me with the power of your holy Presence when I face enemies that seek to distract, deter, or derail your purposes. You have overcome the world (John 16:33).

Knowing that you are aware of all things before they occur, I praise you for wisdom to turn to you quickly when I face distressing situations. Thank you for shining the blazing light of your truth onto the confusion of deceit, callousness, and cruelty. Thank you for reminding me that you sometimes call me into dark places to be a light in your name.

I praise you for teaching me that every conflict has spiritual roots. Thank you for providing a way to access supernatural power to preempt or engage those who come against me spiritually, physically, or emotionally:

- ✳ the power of prayer (James 4:1–3).
- ✳ faith in your authority and goodness (2 Peter 1:3).
- ✳ knowledge of your scripture (Ephesians 6:17).

Lord Jesus, thank you for calling on me to love and pray for my enemies as you loved and prayed for those who crucified you. Thank you for drawing me to yourself when I was your enemy—when I rebelled against you and turned my back on your Spirit's direction. Your agenda was never to save yourself but to lay down your life for me. What undeniable compassion, mercy, and hope you pour into me!

Thank you for the ability to stand strong
in faith today and give myself fully to your work,
knowing that you are accomplishing good purposes
that will last for eternity (1 Corinthians 15:58).

In the name of Jesus, I pray. Amen.

Establish

*I will declare that your love stands firm forever, that you
have established your faithfulness in heaven itself.*
Psalm 89:2

*Commit to the LORD whatever you do, and
he will establish your plans.*
Proverbs 16:3

*And I pray that you, being rooted and established in love,
may have power, together with all the Lord's holy people, to
grasp how wide and long and high and deep is the love of
Christ and to know this love that surpasses knowledge—that
you may be filled to the measure of all the fullness of God.*
Ephesians 3:17–19

Ever-Present God,

I honor you today as the Creator of all that exists: every creature and
its habitat, all seasons and everything that grows, the sun, and the
stars. All things were established by you and are sustained by you.
By your choice, you continue to give life—reconciling and raising
up your human creation to share in the celebration of life with you.

As I begin to grasp how purposeful and complete is your care for me,
I thank you for calling me into your family and establishing my role
in your good work. I am grateful that nothing in my past or present
can tear down what you have built or destroy your eternal plans.

Thank you for *intentionally* planting me here, in your history, watching over me, and fulfilling your plans through me. In new opportunities, setbacks, and seasons of success, I praise you as the One who bestows skill, motivation, and advantage.

You are my core and my Cornerstone. Thank you for establishing a covenant of love between us, not casually, but deliberately. Our relationship of faithfulness was accomplished by you, for me, at great, sacrificial cost to yourself. Thank you for wiping clean my record of failures and entrusting me with life's most important assignment—to tell what you have done for me.

I am grateful today that I am established and cherished
by you, my unshakable foundation.
I am not adrift—I am anchored.
I am not alone—I am appointed.
I have a mission. I am equipped. I am loved.
I am yours.

Thank you, my God. In the name of Jesus, I pray. Amen.

Faith

He got up and rebuked the wind and the raging waters;
the storm subsided, and all was calm. "Where is your
faith?" he asked his disciples. In fear and amazement
they asked one another, "Who is this? He commands
even the winds and the water, and they obey him."
Luke 8:24–25

So then, just as you received Christ Jesus as Lord, continue to
live your lives in him, rooted and built up in him, strengthened in
the faith as you were taught, and overflowing with thankfulness.
Colossians 2:6–7

God Over All,

I praise you today as the intensely interested and thoughtfully intervening God. As I draw near to you, I am consumed by your Spirit's peace and joy. Thank you for calling me to an extraordinary *life built on faith*—real confidence—not blind or emotion-driven wishful thinking but an understanding of life with you at its center.

Thank you for teaching me to run *to* you, not *from* you, when things get tough. When the genuineness of my faith is tested, I praise you for your refining work—like gold in fire—that cannot be achieved on an easy path.

I am grateful that your power is available any time to give me all I need as I walk through the realities of heartbreak, harsh people, and hard choices (2 Peter 1:3). Thank you for inviting me to trust you.

As you lovingly listen to me and strengthen me, I praise you for reminding me that your wisdom is higher than even the good things in my limited vision.

Thank you for weaving reminders of your character *throughout this day.* As I acknowledge that you are all-powerful, purehearted, and worthy of my confidence, I am grateful to see you rewrite my worldview and reorder my priorities.

God of all power and wisdom, as your child, I am grateful to live in your favor forever. Thank you for rescuing me from an empty soul-life through the blood of Christ and today giving me the Spirit-filled confidence and commitment to live under your loving command.

Thank you for showing me that even tiny seeds of trust
have great value in your sight.
So, when I step out in faith, I am standing
on the foundation of your faithfulness.

In the name of Jesus, I pray. Amen.

Faithful God

He is the Rock, his works are perfect, and all his ways are just.
A faithful God who does no wrong, upright and just is he.
Deuteronomy 32:4

Know therefore that the LORD your God is God; he is the
faithful God, keeping his covenant of love to a thousand
generations of those who love him and keep his commandments.
Deuteronomy 7:9

Therefore, since we have been justified through faith, we have
peace with God through our Lord Jesus Christ, through whom we
have gained access by faith into this grace in which we now stand.
Romans 5:1–2

God Who Holds My Future,

You are constant, loyal, and unquenchable: my flawlessly Faithful God. Thank you for the gift of faith—the soul-anchoring, peace-inspiring confidence that you are, in fact, the Truth I long for and the Love I was created to share.

As you flood my soul with your light, I praise you as the Creator of the earth within my gaze and the designer of heaven, a place beyond my comprehension (1 Corinthians 2:9).

Thank you for awakening my soul to understand and embrace your power and purposes. I am in awe of your work throughout time: as your people sought you in faith, you have conquered kingdoms, enforced justice, fulfilled promises, closed the mouths of deadly lions, and turned weakness and reluctance into strength.

Thank you for teaching me to turn first to you, with faith not only in your intervention but in your love, so that whatever the outcome, I am able to pray from my heart for your will to be done.

Lord Jesus, thank you for assuring me that you are "the same yesterday and today and forever" (Hebrews 13:8). How secure, steady, and courageous I feel surrounded by your faithfulness!

As I walk through this day with you,
I thank you for reminding me
that I am in your hands, now and forever.
I am so grateful that, even now,
you are fulfilling your promise
to accompany, counsel, discipline, direct,
and encircle me with everlasting love,
my faithful God.

In the name of Jesus, I pray. Amen.

Faithful Life

The life I now live in the body, I live by faith in the Son
of God, who loved me and gave himself for me.
Galatians 2:20

"If you love me, keep my commands."
John 14:15

"Love the Lord your God with all your heart and with
all your soul and with all your mind and with all your
strength. The second is this: Love your neighbor as yourself.
There is no commandment greater than these."
Mark 12:30–31

God of My Life,

I am in awe of you today, the One who *is* Almighty, who *is* Love, who *is* the Fountain of Living Water. Thank you for making your home in my heart and lifting my soul to a life far more abundant than I could envision or design.

Thank you for calling and setting me apart—not to be what is typical in the world but to be intentionally dedicated to shining your goodness. I praise you for instilling new priorities, so that honoring you overwhelms the desire for my own accomplishments or acclaim.

I am grateful to know that your top priority for me, this day, is to love you and show my love by obedience—to do everything in awareness of you and in love for you. Thank you for calling me to surrender the day to your purposes:

- ✳ to ask you to prepare the path before me.
- ✳ to know that wisdom from you is available as I am attentive to your Spirit.
- ✳ to offer praise for successes and repentance for failures and the ability to move forward in confidence.

Thank you for sending me out with incredible power. As I **speak your name**, calmness replaces chaos. As I **call to mind** your eternal authority and goodness, my mind and heart become saturated with the promised influence of your Spirit: "love, joy, peace, forbearance, kindness, goodness, faithfulness, gentleness and self-control" (Galatians 5:22–23).

> Thank you for a new identity and reputation,
> and for the surprising current of joy
> that now runs through my soul.
> I am grateful today to be yours: trusting, training,
> and walking in step with you.
>
> In the name of Jesus, I pray. Amen.

Fear

God is our refuge and strength, an ever-present help in
trouble. Therefore we will not fear, though the earth give
way and the mountains fall into the heart of the sea.
Psalm 46:1–2

I sought the LORD and he answered me; he delivered
me from all my fears. Those who look to him are
radiant; their faces are never covered with shame.
Psalm 34:4–6

God Who Steadies Me,

You are my Security, my Shield—Almighty God who surrounds me.
As this fact filters into my heart, I am in reverent respect of your
authority over the world and over my fear. I honor you today as the
Sovereign God. You hold the power to create or to dismantle any
action, intention, or force.

> *"There is no wisdom, no insight, no plan that*
> *can succeed against the LORD."*
> Proverbs 21:30

I am so grateful that I do not have to waste another moment dreading
what could happen, but I can rejoice in your precious, courage-
inspiring words: "So do not fear, for I am with you" (Isaiah 41:10).

Thank you for inviting me to rely on you through daunting paths where the outcome is known only to you—praying for my heart's desire and trusting that your higher purposes will prevail.

Thank you for reminding me today that you are my life's Anchor and solid Foundation. In your Presence, I find my confidence and wholeness.

> ❋ In conflict there is deep calm (John 14:27).
> ❋ In loss there is still love (1 Chronicles 16:34).
> ❋ In weakness your power is most evident (2 Corinthians 4:7).

Thank you for teaching me to approach each challenge with worship—to deliberately remember that you are the perfect, all-powerful Creator and Sustainer, the God of all wisdom, and the One who calls me by name (Psalm 50:14-15).

Thank you for holding me close and
inviting me to pour out my heart
to you, relaxing and releasing my emotions
in the safety of your arms.
When I call your name, you bring truth and hope to mind,
and a deep river of peace runs through my soul.
Thank you, Lord, my Strength and Overcoming One.

In the name of Jesus, I pray. Amen.

Finish

I make known the end from the beginning, from
ancient times, what is still to come. I say, "My purpose
will stand, and I will do all that I please."
Isaiah 46:10

"My food," said Jesus, "is to do the will of him
who sent me and to finish his work."
John 4:34

When he had received the drink, Jesus said, "It is finished."
With that, he bowed his head and gave up his spirit.
John 19:30

God Who Watches Over Me,

I honor you as the Eternal, All-Knowing Supreme Authority: you live outside of time and rule over time. You are the Source of all hope and the One who fulfills your good plans. Whatever you start, you finish.

I honor you, Lord Jesus, as the "author and finisher of our faith" (Hebrews 12:2 KJV). I praise you for your life's work: to wrap me in your righteousness and bring me with great joy into our Father's kingdom. Because I am secured in you, God sees me-*in*-you—and heaven celebrates (Luke 15:10).

Thank you for a new heart and a new future guided and guarded by you (1 John 1:8). How reassuring it is to know that whether I'm thrown into chaos or cruise a clear and easy road, you are here and you are mine. Your faultless, unfailing love triumphs.

I praise you for calling me to a life mission that I cannot achieve by myself, so it is evident that power to accomplish your purposes comes from you (2 Corinthians 4:7). Thank you for teaching me that your definition of finishing well is not the world's view of influence or success—it is higher and more meaningful than the life goals I could envision on my own.

Thank you for reminding me today that I am planted in your Presence. My soul's assignment is to flourish and bear good *fruit for the rest of my life* as I proclaim your lovingkindness.

> Thank you for sending me out today
> to season my surroundings
> with encouragement and hope,
> "being confident of this,
> that he who began a good work in you
> will carry it on to completion
> until the day of Christ Jesus" (Philippians 1:6).

In your powerful name, Lord Jesus, I praise and pray, knowing I will one day see your perfect purposes fulfilled. Amen.

Follow Me

He calls his own sheep by name and leads them out. When he has brought out all his own, he goes on ahead of them, and his sheep follow him because they know his voice.
John 10:3–4

"Whoever does not take up their cross and follow me is not worthy of me. Whoever finds their life will lose it, and whoever loses their life for my sake will find it."
Matthew 10:38–39

Therefore, I urge you, brothers and sisters, in view of God's mercy, to offer your bodies as a living sacrifice, holy and pleasing to God—this is your true and proper worship.
Romans 12:1

My Good Shepherd,

Thank you for calling me by name. What a privilege and joy it is to release myself into your will and say, "Here I am, ready to follow." Thank you for summoning me to lay down my own desires and become a living sacrifice that is holy and pleasing to you.

Thank you for welcoming me into your Presence to worship you throughout the day, and for drawing me so close that my love for you outweighs the cost of following you. Even when those around me doubt, aim arrows of unbelief at my soul, or point to the brokenness of the world and my own imperfection as reasons to dismiss faith, I thank you for reminding me that you are the Creator, Sustainer, and

Redeemer. Only through your Spirit can I understand the brokenness of sin reflected in nature, our bodies, and our souls. Only in your Presence can I experience grace and hope.

Lord Jesus, thank you for inviting me to fix my eyes on you, my leader and life example. As you taught and healed, your focus remained steadily on God's ultimate purpose: to rescue and restore us at the cost of your life. Thank you for praying, "Not my will, but yours be done" (Luke 22:42).

I am grateful that specific situations bring opportunities to explore your will by turning to your Word and listening to your Spirit. The more I follow, the more I see you lead.

Father, thank you for planting a desire to be vigilant in my heart and mind. The more intentionally I look to you, the easier and more natural it becomes to let go of lesser, insignificant things including worry and negative thoughts.

Your Presence restores my soul.
So, when everything else demands my attention, I thank you
for reminding me to run to you first and throughout the day,
my True, Faithful Teacher and Gracious Guide.

In the name of Jesus, I pray. Amen.

Forgiven

In him we have redemption through his blood, the
forgiveness of sins, in accordance with the riches
of God's grace that he lavished on us.
Ephesians 1:7–8

If you, LORD, kept a record of sins,
Lord, who could stand?
But with you there is forgiveness,
so that we can, with reverence, serve you.
Psalm 130:3

Restore to me the joy of your salvation and
grant me a willing spirit, to sustain me.
Psalm 51:12

God Who Makes a Way,

I am amazed at the depth of your mercy, kindness, and rescuing power. Thank you for making peace between us—not just tolerance but genuine care and welcoming favor.

Lord Jesus, when I consider the cost of forgiveness, I am overwhelmed by your love and determination to save and heal my soul. You sacrificed yourself on the cross for me, *exchanging your holiness for my sin.* Thank you for opening my soul to believe and receive this gift and for revealing what your love really means: *You hold nothing against me.*

❋ You have saved me from hell: eternal misery that comes from separation from you and all that is good.
❋ You have replaced my rebellion with peace and covered my shame with righteousness and approval.
❋ You have made yourself at home in my heart and prepared a place for me to live with you forever in love, joy, and peace that exceed my imagination.

Thank you for surrounding me with tender forgiveness and hope when I come face-to-face with the consequences of my sin. You are in the battle with me, making a way from destruction to soul healing. As I stand in the light of your Presence, I am grateful to realize that *this* is your plan for me:

❋ the relief of forgiveness and wholeness (Colossians 1:13–14).
❋ the assurance and freedom of trust (Proverbs 3:5-6; Galatians 5:1).
❋ wholehearted love *from* you and *for* you (1 John 4:16–19).

As your Spirit sweeps through my soul and heals my emotions,
I am grateful for the vibrant heart-freedom
only available through your intervening hand.
In your welcoming Presence, I celebrate a new level
of obedience, closeness, and peace.

In the name of Jesus, I praise and pray. Amen.

Forgiving Others

When they came to the place called the Skull,
they crucified him there,
along with the criminals—
one on his right, the other on his left.
Jesus said, "Father, forgive them,
for they do not know what they are doing."
Luke 23:33–34

Bear with each other and forgive one another
if any of you has a grievance against someone.
Forgive as the Lord forgave you.
Colossians 3:13

My Compassionate God,

As I come face-to-face with my own sin and your sacrifice, I am grateful for grace and strength to forgive those who hurt me. I am so glad that you are my Wonderful Counselor and the One who loves me unconditionally. Thank you for inviting me to fully release my grief, anger, and confusion within the safety of your almighty arms.

※ Thank you for teaching me not to skim over pain or pretend that wrong is right, but to bring it to you, the One with ultimate authority over my life and the lives of those who have harmed me.

✳ Thank you for freeing me from resentment and my desire to get even by walking me into forgiveness and the relief, tranquility, and joy you bring.

Loving God, thank you for releasing my heart from a focus on blame, and instead, commanding me to pray for those who have wronged me. Thank you for sharing the burden of my sorrow and not allowing unforgiveness to rule over me.

All-Powerful God, thank you for sending me out as a person of peace with a mission to bless, not curse, and to preempt and react to evil with good (Romans 12:14–21). Thank you for the privilege of serving you, Lord, as one of the most influential, Christlike examples my opponents may ever encounter.

My Savior, I am so grateful that you not only forgive,
but also transform my thinking to reflect your heart.
Thank you for filling my soul with your light
so that—out of the overflow of gratitude in my life—
I can offer godly forgiveness
that is heartfelt, deliberate, and free.

In the name of Jesus, I pray. Amen.

Generous

But when the kindness and love of God our Savior appeared,
he saved us, not because of righteous things we had done,
but because of his mercy. He saved us through the washing
of rebirth and renewal by the Holy Spirit, whom he poured
out on us generously through Jesus Christ our Savior.
Titus 3:4–6

And God is able to bless you abundantly, so that
in all things at all times, having all that you need,
you will abound in every good work.
2 Corinthians 9:8

Abundant God,

I am grateful for the generous love of your Spirit. Your word washes over me like a refreshing wave, and I bask in the sunlight of your Presence. I enjoy you. I praise you for giving me life and drawing me to yourself through Jesus, opening the senses of my soul to experience the depth of your sustaining power and the delight of your company.

Everything in heaven and earth is yours. As I savor your abundant creation and life-giving Presence, I am overwhelmed with the realization that you, the True and Living God, intentionally set my life in motion and continue to pour out more blessings than my finite mind can comprehend.

I praise you as my generous Provider, my invincible Protector, and my constant Friend. You are the One who holds the keys to life and unveils rich knowledge and wisdom available only in your Presence.

Thank you for showering me with every spiritual blessing in Christ.

- ❋ I am chosen and loved with everlasting love (Ephesians 1:4–6).
- ❋ It is your pleasure and will to live in me (Luke 12:32; Romans 15:13).
- ❋ I am understood, and I am given your Spirit to discern what is good and wise (James 1:5; Colossians 3:16).
- ❋ Your love, joy, and peace are working in me to produce godly patience and consistent self-control (Galatians 5:22–23).

Thank you for your command to be open-hearted and open-handed as your generosity flows through me.

In joy and gratitude, I embrace the holy calling
to nurture the people around me
with the attention and kindness that your Spirit inspires in me
this day, in this opportunity, in your love.

In the name of Jesus, I pray. Amen.

Genuine

For the word of the L<small>ORD</small> is right and
true; he is faithful in all he does.
Psalm 33:4

In all this you greatly rejoice, though now for a little while you
may have had to suffer grief in all kinds of trials. These have
come so that the proven genuineness of your faith—of greater
worth than gold, which perishes even though refined by fire—may
result in praise, glory and honor when Jesus Christ is revealed.
1 Peter 1:6–7

My Trustworthy God,

"How excellent is Your name in all the earth" (Psalm 8:1 NKJV). I honor you today as the only God: my hope in this life and my eternal future. You alone possess absolute, reliable Truth. I praise you today, remembering that your care is genuine, your Word is valid, and your character is perfect.

You are Omniscient: As the All-Knowing One, you thoroughly comprehend every event and motivation of my past, present, and future (Hebrews 4:12–13). I am deeply glad to be genuinely known and gladly received by you.

You are Omnipotent: You are the One who designed all things and holds all power (Ephesians 1:18–21). I am thankful, in this moment, to be included in your creation and held in your authority.

You are Omnipresent: You are everywhere, watching, and involved in your world with your eternal purposes in mind. Thank you for revealing your unchanging promises.

✳ You say your love endures forever, *and it does* (Psalm 118:1).
✳ You say you will provide a way out when I face temptation, *and you do* (1 Corinthians 10:13).
✳ You say you will bless me with everything I need to live in challenging circumstances, *and you do* (2 Corinthians 12:9; 2 Peter 1:3).
✳ You say that your sacrifice on the cross covers all my sins, and I am embraced in your forever family, *and I am* (Hebrews 10:10; 1 Peter 3:18).

Thank you for the genuine wholeness—the profound soul-health—
I find in you alone. You are my fulfillment.
You are my security. You are my well-being.
I am grateful to walk through this day with you,
my Sovereign God and life's true Companion.

In the name of Jesus, I pray. Amen.

Government

*The Son is the image of the invisible God, the firstborn
over all creation. For in him all things were created:
things in heaven and on earth, visible and invisible,
whether thrones or powers or rulers or authorities; all
things have been created through him and for him.*
Colossians 1:15–16

*I urge, then, first of all, that petitions, prayers, intercession
and thanksgiving be made for all people—for kings
and all those in authority, that we may live peaceful
and quiet lives in all godliness and holiness.*
1 Timothy 2:1–2

God Over All,

I praise you as the ultimate authority: our Life-Giver and Sustainer. All things exist and continue by your will. By your hand, day follows night, nations rise and fall, and leaders gain and relinquish power.

Thank you for the holy assignment of praying for those in government positions, from the highest to the lowliest places of service. Only you can infuse leadership with righteousness and the skill and will to govern with godliness.

I am so grateful for freedom to gather in your name and worship you. Thank you for opening hearts and doors of opportunity as you reveal your truth and call us to acknowledge *you as Sovereign.*

Thank you for empowering me today with strength and compassion to genuinely love my neighbors and live honorably so that I am a joy, not a burden, to those who lead me and those within my authority. I recognize—in joy, confidence, and humble gratitude—that you are my highest authority, and you promise to bring wisdom as I seek to act with godly integrity in my sphere of influence.

As you lead us all through this season of life, I praise you for inviting me to pray for divine guidance among those who govern—for insight, vision, and transformation that surpass human ability as they look to you. Thank you for examples of your power and love throughout history. Under the covering of your great mercy, you are even able to unite opposing groups and replace hate with genuine, selfless care (Genesis 45:3–7; Philippians 4:7).

I praise you most of all, Lord Jesus, for your life
and sacrificial death—the supreme model of servant leadership.
I honor you as the risen Christ and welcome your return
as you bring about a new heaven and new earth
"where righteousness dwells" (2 Peter 3:13)
under your complete, perfect rule.

In your name, Lamb of God, I pray. Amen.

Grace

Therefore, since we have been justified through faith, we have peace with God through our Lord Jesus Christ, through whom we have gained access by faith into this grace in which we now stand.
Romans 5:1–2

For it is by grace you have been saved, through faith—and this is not from yourselves, it is the gift of God—not by works, so that no one can boast.
Ephesians 2:8–9

Let us then approach God's throne of grace with confidence, so that we may receive mercy and find grace to help us in our time of need.
Hebrews 4:16

God Who Welcomes Me,

In this holy moment, I pause to absorb the wonder of *who you are:* my grace-filled Maker, God-Who-Sees-Me. I honor you as the Righteous Judge, a Consuming Fire against evil, my Advocate, and the Living God who is my Peace.

Thank you for revealing that your favor—your grace—is something that I can never earn. It is freely given from your heart. How tenderly and lovingly you view my life! How willing you are to release the full force of your grace to accomplish things otherwise impossible.

Lord Jesus, I praise you for taking thousands of years of humanity's sin on yourself and exchanging it for your righteousness. No cost, time, or effort on your part was too great a sacrifice to bring me into your Presence. Knowing the misery of sin before I could comprehend it, you compassionately drew me to yourself to rescue me from hell and heal my broken soul. And your grace continues:

※ grace for the many, many times you have spared me from the consequences of my rebellious, naïve, or thoughtless choices.

※ grace when the reality of this fallen world hits head-on with loss and grief—when you are with me in the storm.

I am grateful today that I am not meant to walk alone: you intend for me, your cherished creation, to walk *with you,* to share life *with you,* and to work *with you* in surprising those around me with heartfelt grace.

Today, as you flood my soul with the power of your Spirit,
I thank you for providing everything I need
to bless the culture with grace, hope, and heart-healing
that flow from your throne.

In the name of Jesus, I pray. Amen.

Grief

But you, God, see the trouble of the afflicted; you
consider their grief and take it in hand.
Psalm 10:14

"To give them beauty for ashes,
The oil of joy for mourning,
The garment of praise for the spirit of heaviness;
That they may be called trees of righteousness,
The planting of the LORD, that He may be glorified."
Isaiah 61:3 (NKJV)

But those who hope in the LORD will renew their strength.
They will soar on wings like eagles; they will run and
not grow weary, they will walk and not be faint.
Isaiah 40:31

God My Firm Foundation,

You are steadfast, loyal, and always present. I praise you today as my Anchor. When my earthly foundation seems to crumble in crisis, you remain my Refuge, Rescuer, and Strength. As I inhale this reality, I am overwhelmed by your loving Presence. You are my Comforter and my unwavering Sustainer: the One who carries me.

Thank you for inviting me to pour out my heart to you, knowing that you tenderly grieve with me and hold me through the sorrow.

I am so grateful for your promise to never leave me. I do not have to navigate the future blindly; you chart the path ahead of me and bring peace that transcends trials. I praise you for the tranquility of your Spirit—not just an absence of penetrating hurt but a waterfall of relief that sweeps me into its life-giving current.

Thank you for bringing a new perspective—a celebration of your saving power and a reminder that only you are my soul's permanent, perfect dwelling place. Since you experienced death for my sins and resurrection to new life, I live today in forward-looking faith and the knowledge that I am in your hands. Thank you for reminding me of everything you have promised: that you will empower, counsel, encourage, and bring discernment.

Thank you for drawing me close so that grief is bathed in hope, and sorrow is saturated with anticipation of my future with you: my light, my love, and my eternal life.

In the name of Jesus, I pray. Amen.

Heart

Since, then, you have been raised with Christ, set your hearts
on things above, where Christ is, seated at the right hand of
God. Set your minds on things above, not on earthly things.
For you died, and your life is now hidden with Christ in God.
Colossians 3:1–3

May these words of my mouth
and this meditation of my heart
be pleasing in your sight, LORD,
my Rock and my Redeemer.
Psalm 19:14

God Who Fills My Heart,

I am so grateful that you are mine, and your love endures *forever.*
Your heart pours into my heart a river of life-giving strength and
wholeness. As I set my gaze on you, I begin to grasp the weight of
your promises: I can trust you with everything I am and everything
I need.

I praise you because your decisions flow from your perfect
character—your complete insight and your compassion—and there
is a good purpose in your heart for everything you do. This releases
me from anxiety and fills me with profound and permanent peace.

I praise you for reconstructing my heart to reflect your honor and
ability to discern truth. Thank you for reaching into the undiscovered

depths of my soul to bring sin and shame to the surface of my thinking—the shadowy places that need your transforming touch.

I am in awe of your power to replace heart-heaviness with a pure heart (Psalm 51:10–12). When you say my heart is clean, *it is clean,* and I can embrace this new reality with purpose and joy.

Thank you for teaching me that praising and honoring you is God-given food for the soul. I am not to starve my spirit by ignoring your goodness or marinating on the imperfect and hurtful but to feast on the foundational knowledge of your self-sacrificing love.

Thank you for storing up good things in my heart
so that the accumulation of your Word
and the work of your Spirit
cause true and encouraging things
to fill my soul
and flow out of my mouth.

"My heart leaps for joy, and with my song I praise him"
(Psalm 28:7).

In the name of Jesus, I pray. Amen.

Heartache

*Trust in him at all times, you people; pour out
your hearts to him, for God is our refuge.*
Psalm 62:8

*Surely He has borne our griefs
And carried our sorrows.*
Isaiah 53:4 (NKJV)

*May our Lord Jesus Christ himself and God our
Father, who loved us and by his grace gave us eternal
encouragement and good hope, encourage your hearts
and strengthen you in every good deed and word.*
2 Thessalonians 2:16–17

My Loving God,

You are my Life. Your Presence far outweighs the influence of
other people, events, and circumstances. *You are my God—forever.*
Knowing that I am surrounded by your deep and lasting love, I can
face heartache head-on. I am so grateful for the assurance that you
are not surprised or powerless in my situation but walking ahead and
carrying me through this season.

I praise you today as my source of strength, wisdom, and courage.
Lord Jesus, thank you for reminding me that you also mourned over
loss and rejection. Thank you for calling me to pray for those who
choose a path of destructive rebellion and "pierce themselves"—and
me—with grief (1 Timothy 6:9–10). And whether you change the

source of heartache now or allow it to run its course, I look forward to seeing the ultimate purpose you are bringing (Romans 8:26–28). In the meantime, I praise you for saturating me with your truth. Thank you for...

> **Love** that is intense and enduring, so that I "may have power, together with all the Lord's holy people, to grasp how wide and long and high and deep is the love of Christ" (Ephesians 3:18).

> **Confidence** and **delight** in your Presence. "The LORD is my strength and my shield; my heart trusts in him" (Psalm 28:7).

> **Peace** that calms and counsels me. "And the peace of God, which transcends all understanding, will guard your hearts and your minds in Christ Jesus" (Philippians 4:7).

My God, how precious you are to me! Thank you for inviting me to walk through this day surrounded by your soul-lifting Spirit. Thank you for holding me in your heart, now and for eternity.

In the name of Jesus, I pray. Amen.

Heaven

After this I heard what sounded like the roar of a great multitude
in heaven shouting: "Hallelujah! Salvation and glory and power
belong to our God, for true and just are his judgments."
Revelation 19:1–2

"Do not let your hearts be troubled. You believe in God; believe
also in me. My Father's house has many rooms; if that were not
so, would I have told you that I am going there to prepare a place
for you? And if I go to prepare a place for you, I will come back
and take you to be with me that you also may be where I am."
John 14:1–3

My Welcoming God,

Thank you for giving me "new birth into a living hope through the resurrection of Jesus Christ from the dead, and into an inheritance that can never perish, spoil or fade" (1 Peter 1:3–4). Today, I join the thousands and thousands of angels in heaven celebrating the reality that you have rescued my soul and made me righteous and acceptable—and you joyfully await the day when you will embrace me in the heavenly home you have prepared for me.

Thank you for teaching me to keep heaven always in my view and to gratefully anticipate the day when "I shall know fully, even as I am fully known" (1 Corinthians 13:12). You are my inheritance, my future, and my fulfillment.

Creator of heaven and earth, thank you for drawing me close and enabling me to experience a taste of your goodness now as your Spirit floods me with love, joy, and peace. I praise you for preparing me for the day when you fulfil your promises:

⁜ to banish death and pain so there is no need for tears from my eyes or mourning from my heart (Revelation 21:1–4).

⁜ to bring a new heaven and new earth free of harm, hostility, or impurity and illuminated by the light of your magnificent, loving Presence (Revelation 21:22–27).

Lord Jesus, you are Faithful and True. Thank you for writing my name in your Book of Life (Revelation 21:27).

I am eager to see your face. As I look forward to that day,
I thank you for instructing me to store up treasure in heaven—
in your name to spread love and mercy to the people around me
because *you* are gracious, *you* are Love,
and you freely welcome me.

Lord Jesus, in your holy name I praise and pray. Amen.

Honor

"You are worthy, our Lord and God,
to receive glory and honor and power,
for you created all things,
and by your will they were created
and have their being."
Revelation 4:11

He humbled himself by becoming obedient to death—even
death on a cross! Therefore God exalted him to the highest
place and gave him the name that is above every name, that
at the name of Jesus every knee should bow, in heaven and
on earth and under the earth, and every tongue acknowledge
that Jesus Christ is Lord, to the glory of God the Father.
Philippians 2:8–11

My Living, Loving Lord,

You, alone, are God. You are worthy of worship and adoration. Thank you for teaching me that your very name is holy: not to be used irreverently or casually but with the greatest awe and respect. For the sake of your name—to display and apply your honor—you intervene in power (Psalm 106:8), exercise mercy (Ezekiel 20:44), and eternally preserve your people in faithful love (Isaiah 48:9–11).

I honor you today as my Life Giver and Life Savior. Nothing is more valuable than your Presence. "Yes, everything else is worthless when compared with the priceless gain of knowing Christ Jesus my Lord" (Philippians 3:8 TLB).

Thank you for relentlessly pursuing me, knowing the key to my heart that would unlock my understanding of you, the Light of the World, the Bread of Life, and the Living Water. Thank you for calling on me, this day, to display your purity and wisdom so that the reality of your transforming power inspires many to honor you.

Today, I am grateful for a fresh glimpse of your "excellent greatness" (Psalm 150:2)…

- ✳ as I meditate on your word. How wise and trustworthy are your thoughts (Psalm 119:14).
- ✳ as I absorb the beauty of your creation and remember that you said it was good (Genesis 1:31).
- ✳ as I savor the way that you graciously provide all that I need (Matthew 6:28–33).

Thank you for a heart overflowing with praise—remembering that
you are glad to give us your kingdom (Luke 12:32)
where we will spend eternity honoring you
and rejoicing over you.

In the name of Jesus, I pray. Amen.

I AM

Moses said to God, "Suppose I go to the Israelites and say to them, 'The God of your fathers has sent me to you,' and they ask me, 'What is his name?' Then what shall I tell them?" God said to Moses, "I AM WHO I AM."
Exodus 3:13–14

"I am the Alpha and the Omega," says the Lord God, "who is, and who was, and who is to come, the Almighty."
Revelation 1:8

And he passed in front of Moses, proclaiming, "The LORD, the LORD, the compassionate and gracious God, slow to anger, abounding in love and faithfulness, maintaining love to thousands, and forgiving wickedness, rebellion and sin."
Exodus 34:6

Everlasting God,

Thank you for proclaiming your eternal identity. You have life in and of yourself. You are self-existent and self-sufficient. I honor you today as the One whose existence predates creation and will outlast the earth. Thank you for including me in your work. Because you are, I am.

I am deeply grateful for your desire to be known by humanity—to love and inspire love. I praise you for displaying your character in your design of the universe, so that your power and sustaining care are clearly seen (Romans 1:20).

Because you exist *forever*, your qualities endure: your selfless delight in your children, your compassion, and your faithfulness are mine for eternity.

Lord Jesus, I honor you as God-in-the-flesh, our Rescuing One (John 10:30). I awe and gratitude, I praise you for proclaiming your unparalleled love and continuing care. Thank you for revealing who you are to me.

> ❋ "I am the good shepherd" (John 10:11); "I am the gate; whoever enters through me will be saved" (John 10:9).
> ❋ "I am the resurrection and the life. The one who believes in me will live, even though they die" (John 11:25).
> ❋ "I am the bread of life" (John 6:48).
> ❋ "I am the light of the world" (John 8:12).
> ❋ "I am the vine; you are the branches. If you remain in me and I in you, you will bear much fruit" (John 15:5).
> ❋ "I am the way and the truth and the life. No one comes to the Father except through me" (John 14:6).

Immersed in your holiness, surrounded
by your love, and confident in
your character, I am eternally grateful to belong to you.

In your name, Lord Jesus, I pray and praise. Amen.

Instruction

*I will instruct you and teach you in the way you should
go; I will counsel you with my loving eye on you.*
Psalm 32:8

*Your instructions are more valuable to me than millions
in gold and silver. You made me; you created me. Now
give me the sense to follow your commands.*
Psalm 119:72–73 (NLT)

*What we have received is not the spirit of the world,
but the Spirit who is from God, so that we may
understand what God has freely given us.*
1 Corinthians 2:12

God Who Teaches Me,

In grateful anticipation, I look forward to the treasures of wisdom and insight you are unfolding today. As I consciously commune with you, drawing knowledge and nourishment, I humbly praise you as my Guide and my Counselor. You are the door to deep understanding. You not only provide perception of the world around me but intensely satisfying spiritual truth—things only discerned in your Presence.

Thank you for speaking straight into my soul through scripture. Your words are a feast for me: like bread that sustains me, a fountain that refreshes me, and conviction that cuts deeply to reform and refine me.

Thank you for teaching me through your commands and your history: "They are not just idle words for you—they are your life" (Deuteronomy 32:47). Thank you for revealing your priorities for me:

* ❋ to love you and love others so completely that when self-sacrifice is needed, I am willing (Matthew 22:37–39).
* ❋ to hide your word in my heart so that the difference between right and wrong is clear, and I am able to choose your good path (Psalm 119:11).
* ❋ to align my thinking and direction with yours and find wholeness only in you (1 Peter 2:2–3).

Thank you for your Spirit to lead me through this day—to remind me to bring decisions to you and to reassure me of your constant vigilance.

Thank you for a continuous thirst for understanding
that leads me back to this central truth:
"Know that the LORD is God.
It is he who made us, and we are his"
(Psalm 100:3)

In the name of Jesus, I pray. Amen.

Integrity

All-Wise God,

I praise you today as the One who always keeps your promises—
you alone are completely dependable. Your word stands firm and
trustworthy forever. As I keep my eyes steadfastly on you, I know
I can rely on your flawless integrity: the wisdom and goodwill that
flow through complete knowledge of everything in the past, present,
and future.

I praise you because you never do anything evil or hateful. Even
when I face the hard consequences of my sin or the wrongdoing
of others, you are using my circumstances to work everything for
ultimate good while making me stronger, purer, and more attuned to
you. And as I stand on *your* integrity, I will not be shaken.

Your holiness fills me with confidence and joy. I am in awe of your unique, complete purity. Thank you for infusing me with the desire and ability to "walk in the way of love, just as Christ loved us and gave himself up for us as a fragrant offering and sacrifice to God" (Ephesians 5:1).

As I recount the ways you are faithful to me, my soul celebrates your tireless work to bring honesty and selflessness into my ordinary choices and extraordinary challenges.

I praise you today because—although we live in a fallen world—I can count on your decisions, your plans, and your heart to be faultless. In the glow of your Light, my steps are illuminated, and my direction becomes clear.

I am eternally grateful for your loving, grace-filled integrity
and for leading me, this day, in paths of righteousness
so that my thoughts, intentions, and words
bring honor to you.

In the name of Jesus, I pray. Amen.

Intercede

But because Jesus lives forever, he has a permanent priesthood.
Therefore he is able to save completely those who come to God
through him, because he always lives to intercede for them.
Hebrews 7:24–25

"As for me, far be it from me that I should sin
against the LORD by failing to pray for you. And I
will teach you the way that is good and right."
1 Samuel 12:23

Intervening God,

You are full of mercy: truly, deeply kind. I treasure you as my Defender, Deliverer, and Friend. I praise you as the One who inspires compassion for the people around me so that prayers for deliverance flow naturally from my soul into your powerful Presence.

Lord Jesus, thank you for interceding for me—stepping in to exchange your perfection for my sins. I am so grateful that my past, present, and even future sins are the subject of your intense concern and intervention: "we have an advocate who pleads our case before the Father. He is Jesus Christ, the one who is truly righteous" (1 John 2:1 NLT).

Thank you for your involvement throughout history as you have led your people to pray:

❋ against rebellion and destruction (Numbers 16:42–48).

❋ for protection, forgiveness, and healing (1 Samuel 7:5–9; Mark 5:22–23, 39–42).

❋ for peaceful relationships (Genesis 32:9–11; Genesis 33:4).

❋ for wisdom (1 Kings 3:9; 1 Kings 4:29).

Thank you for showing me that you alone have the power to bring the lasting heart transformation, life choices, and wholeness that I earnestly desire for those around me. I am grateful to know that my assignment is to lay my requests before you, speak truth as you direct me, and relinquish results to your Holy Spirit.

Knowing that your love and power
are far greater than I can comprehend,
I thank you for the privilege of interceding
for the people you place on my path,
and for inviting me to pray, with thanksgiving,
for the good work you have begun
(1 Thessalonians 5:17–18).

In the name of Jesus, I pray. Amen.

Joy

You make known to me the path of life;
you will fill me with joy in your presence,
with eternal pleasures at your right hand.
Psalm 16:11

"As the Father has loved me, so have I loved you. Now
remain in my love. If you keep my commands, you will
remain in my love, just as I have kept my Father's commands
and remain in his love. I have told you this so that my joy
may be in you and that your joy may be complete."
John 15:9–11

God Over All,

I praise you as the Creator of joy and the One who nourishes my soul with gladness (Nehemiah 8:10). Thank you for revealing that you are a joyful being. I am so grateful to know that joy is a key component of your character and a natural outflow of your Spirit.

Even in distressing times, there is relief, release, and the knowledge that the foundational joy of your Spirit is still solid and waiting to seep back into my consciousness—because it is the *joy of your Presence*. It is promised. It is persistent. It is a gift accessible to all believers (Galatians 5:22).

Thank you for designing me to savor your Presence. How refreshing it is to realize that:

❊ You enjoyed designing humanity and now enjoy my company (Genesis 1:27, 31; Luke 12:32).

❊ Even as you endured the suffering and shame of the cross, you focused on the joy of bringing me new life (Hebrews 12:2).

❊ You rejoice over your people with singing and richly provide all things for our enjoyment (Zephaniah 3:17; 1 Timothy 6:17).

Thank you for showing me that joy naturally follows my commitment to keep your commands. In your great compassion, you examine my distracted heart and clean out everything that hinders me from the joy of your Presence (Psalm 51:12).

Today, I worship you with gladness
that filters into every part of this
life you have given me:
*"For the Lord is good
and his love endures forever"*
(Psalm 100:5).

In the name of Jesus, I praise and thank you, amen.

Justice

Righteousness and justice are the foundation of your
throne; love and faithfulness go before you.
Psalm 89:14

He has shown you, O mortal, what is good. And what
does the LORD require of you? To act justly and to
love mercy and to walk humbly with your God.
Micah 6:8

But let justice roll on like a river, righteousness
like a never-failing stream!
Amos 5:24

My Just and Merciful God,

I praise you as the all-knowing, perfect Judge, aware of every thought, plan, and hidden purpose. You are the Righteous One, the Holy One, and the only One with a complete grasp of justice. Nothing escapes your attention: every attitude, motivation and action are open before you (Hebrews 4:12–13).

Thank you for considering justice a precious priority. I am so grateful that you are a refuge for the oppressed, the unjustly criticized, and the mistreated or ignored. Thank you for your promise never to forsake your people.

I praise you for planting a natural desire for justice deep in humanity's heart and for holding me accountable for fairness even when the search for truth and appropriate action is costly. Thank you for your plan to bring ultimate, perfect justice to your cherished world.

All-Knowing One, thank you for not allowing the gut-wrenching burden of revenge to weigh down my heart but teaching me to respect your judgment. Thank you for your assurance that you will avenge evil and accomplish good.

Thank you for infusing your justice with mercy; without your compassion who could survive your righteous judgment (Psalm 130:3–4)? Lord Jesus, thank you for your unfathomable sacrifice: you have paid for my forgiveness with your sinless life to accomplish divine justice and bring righteousness to my soul.

Almighty God, I praise you for the privilege
of joining you in your work to bring justice here and now.
I am grateful that your limitless power—the same mighty strength
that raised Jesus from the dead—is at work in me today
to carry out your holy command to "do to others
as you would have them do to you" (Luke 6:31).

In the name of Jesus, I pray. Amen.

Kindness

The LORD appeared to us in the past, saying: "I have loved you with an everlasting love; I have drawn you with unfailing kindness."
Jeremiah 31:3

But when the kindness and love of God our Savior appeared, he saved us, not because of righteous things we had done, but because of his mercy.
Titus 3:4–5

Therefore, as God's chosen people, holy and dearly loved, clothe yourselves with compassion, kindness, humility, gentleness and patience.
Colossians 3:12

God Who Watches Over Me,

You are my constant companion, my security, and my delight—the One I adore. Thank you for bringing me face-to-face with the knowledge that my life is not my own: I am held, nourished, and blessed by you. I praise you for filtering all things through the awareness of your power and purposes. As I focus on your Presence, your priorities become my priorities, your honor is my motivation, and your grace-filled work drives my day.

Lord Jesus, I am overwhelmed with the knowledge that you are so concerned for my well-being that you gave your life for me. Because you love me *that sincerely*—to sacrifice yourself—I can only fall at your feet in amazement and love.

- ❋ I honor you for caring enough to discipline me as a good father trains his child; your training is an act of kindness and patience (Proverbs 3:11–12).
- ❋ Thank you for calling me to be kind even when the world around me seems out of control and oblivious to your goodness. You are "kind to the ungrateful and the wicked" (Luke 6:35).
- ❋ I praise you for commanding me to shed selfishness in favor of true kindness that expects nothing in return. Thank you for the celebration we share in freely offering good will.

Today, I thank you for drawing my heart to your heart,
valuing our time together and rejoicing in our closeness.
Through your eyes, I experience the reality of love that is patient,
kind, and freely forgiving. And I find my greatest energy and most
tranquil rest in trusting and worshipping you.
I am forever grateful—for your kindness.

In the name of Jesus, I pray. Amen.

Knowing God

I keep asking that the God of our Lord Jesus Christ,
the glorious Father, may give you the Spirit of wisdom
and revelation, so that you may know him better.
Ephesians 1:17

We continually ask God to fill you with the knowledge
of his will through all the wisdom and understanding
that the Spirit gives, so that you may live a life worthy of
the Lord and please him in every way: bearing fruit in
every good work, growing in the knowledge of God.
Colossians 1:9–10

God Most High,

How exhilarating it is to know you, the God of all that exists! Thank you for welcoming me into your heart and home. As a child knows his earthly parent—learning his qualities and copying his behavior—you invite me to absorb your wisdom and witness your work. Thank you for the assurance that your knowledge is complete, and your purposes are good.

Thank you for revealing that knowing *you* is infinitely more important than discovering information or direction. Thank you for making your name—your character and reputation—evident through your creation, your Word, and your Spirit.

- Thank you for calling me to embrace the stunning splendor of your holiness. All your ways are perfect, and all your decisions are righteous.
- I praise you for daily demonstrating love and mercy. In the same breath, I praise you as the God who righteously judges the destructive power and heartbreak of all that is evil and harmful in your world.
- Thank you for the understanding that your strength will give me everything I need for a godly life. The closer I walk with you, the more wholeheartedly my choices reflect your will, so that I am conformed to your image.
- Thank you for calling me by name, walking ahead of me, and caring for me as a shepherd guards and guides his sheep. I am so grateful that you know what I need before I ask—and that you *invite* me to ask so that your Spirit will guide me into right thinking.

The more I know you, the more freely I love you.
Thank you for being my God: my
Commander, my true Companion,
and the Light of my life.

In the name of Jesus, I pray and praise. Amen.

Knowledge

For God, who said, "Let light shine out of darkness,"
made his light shine in our hearts to give us the light of the
knowledge of God's glory displayed in the face of Christ.
2 Corinthians 4:6

And this is my prayer: that your love may abound more and
more in knowledge and depth of insight, so that you may be
able to discern what is best and may be pure and blameless
for the day of Christ, filled with the fruit of righteousness that
comes through Jesus Christ—to the glory and praise of God.
Philippians 1:9–11

All-Knowing God,

I praise you today as the Author of Life and Teacher of Truth: *you hold the keys to all knowledge.* Your thoughts are higher than mine (Isaiah 55:9), and though I may investigate and map my way, you lead me on a more meaningful journey than I could envision.

I praise you for your perfect knowledge. I cannot see the temptations, challenges, and pitfalls ahead, but you are aware of all things, and you stand ready to lovingly guide me. How humbling it is to realize that my hope, security, and wise path are found only in you.

I am in awe of the ways you unfold and withhold knowledge to accomplish your good purposes. I praise you today for disclosing **knowledge to all people** as a means of pointing us to you (Romans 1:20). Thank you for constantly communicating your authority through your creation. I honor you for instilling a desire to comprehend fairness in the world—a hunger to be well-treated even from childhood—so that we seek and find the Source of all knowledge and righteousness.

Thank you for imparting **knowledge to make wise decisions** as I consider your commands. At the beginning of your creation, humanity knew only the goodness of your Presence then chose to become acquainted with evil (Genesis 2:9–3:6)—and the lure of iniquity continues. Thank you for forgiving me when my curiosity entices me into darkness. Thank you for drawing me into your light.

Thank you for allowing me to **discover knowledge step-by-step,**
so that I focus first on you and your holiness
as I pray, work, watch, and wait.

I honor you for reserving some things for you, alone, to know—
including the day when you will end the current world
and bring a new heaven and new earth where I will clearly see
your good and powerful purposes fulfilled.

In the name of Jesus, I pray. Amen.

Lament

Listen to my words, LORD,
consider my lament. Hear my cry for help,
my King and my God, for to you I pray.
Psalm 5:1–2

You, LORD, hear the desire of the afflicted;
you encourage them, and you listen to their cry.
Psalm 10:17

Praise be to the LORD,
for he has heard my cry for mercy.
The LORD is my strength and my shield;
my heart trusts in him, and he helps me.
Psalm 28:6

God Who Listens,

I praise you as my Comforter, Counselor, and Source of Strength. You are the One who sees my distress and shoulders every sorrow. Thank you for inviting me to approach you with honesty.

More than anyone else, you know the source and depth of my pain and unsettled mind. Thank you for speaking your precious promise: "'Come to me, all you who are weary and burdened, and I will give you rest'" (Matthew 11:28).

As I lament *in your Presence*, I am grateful for your wisdom and consolation, and for the assurance that you love me absolutely and eternally. Thank you for lifting me to new heights of trust so that I am not simply complaining but also recognizing who you are.

- ⚘ Your power and insight are able to transform, rescue, and provide. In this fallen world, there will be crises, but you are my Shield and my Shelter (Psalm 18:1–2).
- ⚘ Even though I may feel forsaken, you have promised to be with me always. My wholeness and peace of mind come from you and not my circumstances (Deuteronomy 31:8).
- ⚘ Your unparalleled mercy is woven throughout your work, so that my pleas for intervention can give way to confidence in your goodness and honor (Romans 8:28).

As my grievances become intertwined with praise, I thank you for inviting me to explore and release my emotions in the security of your loving arms.

I am grateful that you *walk through this life with me*
and promise to achieve purposes that have eternal value—
things profoundly beyond my own perception or plans.
Thank you for welcoming me to run to you and rely on you today,
my Good Father, my confidential Friend, and my Deliverer.

In the name of Jesus, I pray. Amen.

Leadership

*Then Jesus came to them and said, "All authority in
heaven and on earth has been given to me."*
Matthew 28:18

*He guides me along the right paths
for his name's sake.*
Psalm 23:3

*Guide me in your truth and teach me, for you are God
my Savior, and my hope is in you all day long.*
Psalm 25:5

Almighty God,

I praise you as the Ruler of the Universe. You are my Good Shepherd,
my Commander, and the One who prepares the way before me.
Thank you for calling me by name and leading me through this day
under your authority. As I respond to my earthly leadership, I am
working for you.

Thank you, Lord Jesus, for assigning me to lead as you have led:
to shine holiness in everyday situations and generously plant godly
ideas, attitudes, and actions in my home and in my work so that *your*
ways may be known.

As I consider your flawless insight and your knowledge of the
past, present, and future, I am grateful for the heartfelt motivation
to submit to the authority you place around me. Thank you for

reminding me to remain attentive to you today so that I will be a joy to lead, a valuable contributor, and a worthy adviser (Hebrews 13:17).

I praise you for calling me to pray for wisdom and selflessness in our leaders—the will and skill to build up rather than tear down. Thank you for commanding me to treat other people as I want to be treated, and to serve as an advocate for the well-being of those around me (Luke 6:31; Ephesians 4:29).

Thank you for greeting me with grace and encouragement when my own leadership falters: when I disobey, act selfishly or carelessly, and make mistakes. Thank you for tenderly placing my feet back on your path with the assurance that you will complete the excellent work you have begun in and around me (Philippians 1:6).

As I devote this day to you—a day you have created—
I thank you for calling me into constant awareness
of your invitation to commune with you.
Thank you for leading me with your understanding,
your promise of wisdom, and your peace.

In the name of Jesus, I pray. Amen.

Listen

*"Very truly I tell you, whoever hears my word and
believes him who sent me has eternal life and will not
be judged but has crossed over from death to life."*
John 5:24

"My sheep listen to my voice; I know them, and they follow me."
John 10:27

*You have declared this day that the LORD is your God and
that you will walk in obedience to him, that you will keep his
decrees, commands and laws—that you will listen to him.*
Deuteronomy 26:17

My Attentive God,

As I hear your name, the warmth of your Spirit saturates my soul.
Thank you for speaking wholeness into me today, reminding me
to stop and breathe in your words. Speak, Lord; I am listening (1
Samuel 3:9–10).

As I draw near to you, listening to your Spirit and your word, I am
grateful to hear the blessings you speak over me.

* ※ "I am with you always" (Matthew 28:20). I am amazed to
  hear that you know every day of my life before it happens.
  So, when you speak comfort or conviction, you speak as the
  One who deeply understands (Psalm 139:16).

❊ "You are the light of the world" (Matthew 5:14). Because you call me to a godly life, you will not leave me helpless in the face of sin, but instead, the *full force of your power* will provide everything I need: wisdom, strength, and courage (1 Peter 1:3).

❊ "My peace I give you" (John 14:27). I am so grateful that you are not opposed to me; you are united with me. As I experience this day in your Presence, the fact that you are good and trustworthy rules my mind, and scripture, not culture, shapes my view of life (John 14:15–17).

Loving God, thank you for prompting me to listen to you throughout this day. How countless and precious are your thoughts to me! As I wait for your direction—whether holding my breath in apprehension or eager anticipation—I thank you for drawing me close enough to hear your heart.

Thank you for replenishing my soul and reminding me
that your life-giving Spirit is always available
to listen and lift my face to you,
my Bread of Life and Living Water.

In the name of Jesus, I praise and pray. Amen.

Love

But God demonstrates his own love for us in this:
While we were still sinners, Christ died for us.
Romans 5:8

"Greater love has no one than this: to lay
down one's life for one's friends."
John 15:13

Surely your goodness and love
will follow me all the days of my life,
and I will dwell in the house
of the LORD forever.
Psalm 23:6

My Devoted God,

Because you exist, love exists. I praise you because your love is deeper than I have imagined and more permeating, more active, and more directly involved than I can comprehend. At the core of your being is love that infuses every interaction and carves every path.

You *are* love—pure love, real love. I honor you for the high priority you place on our closeness. Thank you for revealing your plans for me in your most important commandment: to love you with all my heart, soul, mind, and strength and to actively love my neighbor (Matthew 22:36–40; Luke 10:27).

As the reality of your compassion dawns on my soul, I thank you for…

❋ love that is **intentional**: You designed me in your own image with the capacity and desire for love. I can only love because you created me for love and drew me to yourself.

❋ love that **intervenes**: You are Immanuel—God-With-Us (Matthew 1:23). I praise you as the perfect Judge with the ability to see and crush the things that rob our souls of love: rebellion, stubborn self-focus, and callousness.

❋ love that **unites**: Thank you for taking extreme measures to reconcile us. You have rescued me from the torment of hell—life immersed in evil without you and without hope. But more importantly, you have given me life in the delight of your Presence: *we are together now and forever.*

Encircled in the sacred safety of your love,
I thank you for giving me a life purpose:
to lock my gaze on you so that loving wholeheartedly
and serving sacrificially define my days—
as your love flows into me and through me.

In the name of Jesus, I pray. Amen.

Meditate

*One generation commends your works to another; they tell of
your mighty acts. They speak of the glorious splendor of your
majesty—and I will meditate on your wonderful works.*
Psalm 145:4–5

*You keep him in perfect peace whose mind is
stayed on you, because he trusts in you.*
Isaiah 26:3 (ESV)

*Finally, brothers and sisters, whatever is true, whatever
is noble, whatever is right, whatever is pure, whatever
is lovely, whatever is admirable—if anything is excellent
or praiseworthy—think about such things.*
Philippians 4:8

All-Knowing God,

I praise you for revealing that all creation was designed with *you* at
its center—to relate to you and rely on you. I am thankful to step
into this day with confidence, knowing that your light and power
will shine through me as I meditate on your character: *"The LORD
is compassionate and gracious, slow to anger, abounding in love"*
(Psalm 103:8). I am grateful to know that I never think alone. As I
ponder in your Presence, your Spirit actively engages my thoughts
and often leads me in unexpected directions: unearthing sin, pushing
for or against my plans, and multiplying my faith.

Lord Jesus, thank you for cultivating a habit of meditation *on your character*: you are my most valued treasure (2 Corinthians 4:7), my hope (1 Peter 1:3), and my future (Romans 15:13). You are flawlessly above all humanity, and only in your Presence can I walk in the purity you have given me. I praise you for your unparalleled authority. You have the ability to create or destroy, yet you choose to save. I honor you as the One who watches over me. When I walk through confusion, opposition, or even the shadow of death, I fear no evil (Psalm 23:4).

Thank you for calling me to meditate on your scripture, "proclaiming your love in the morning and your faithfulness at night" (Psalm 92:5)…

* ❈ so that my thoughts are absorbed with your goodness rather than the words of toxic people (Psalm 1:1–3).
* ❈ so that divine insight rules my decisions (Psalm 119:1).
* ❈ so that I am constantly aware that you are with me (Joshua 1:8–9).

As I meditate on your saving, renewing actions of the past,
I look forward to the wonders to come
with your Spirit living and working in me.

In the name of Jesus, I pray. Amen.

Mercy

Praise be to the God and Father of our Lord Jesus Christ! In his great mercy he has given us new birth into a living hope through the resurrection of Jesus Christ from the dead, and into an inheritance that can never perish, spoil or fade.
1 Peter 1:3–4

This is what the LORD Almighty said: "Administer true justice; show mercy and compassion to one another."
Zechariah 7:9

But the wisdom that comes from heaven is first of all pure; then peace-loving, considerate, submissive, full of mercy and good fruit, impartial and sincere.
James 3:17

God Who Watches Over Me,

I am deeply moved by your mercy—not only thoughts of sympathy but intense concern and sacrificial action. With a fresh sense of your compassion, I honor you today for mercy that is both powerful and tender; it is undeserved but wholeheartedly, freely given.

Because you want to immerse me in your precious Presence, you have included my sin in your atoning work. Thank you for replacing my careless attitude toward you with a fervent desire to be intentionally aware of you throughout this day, seeking your wisdom and seeing the world through your grace-filled eyes.

As I reluctantly face the reality that I have sinned and have no remedy to save myself from hell, I am astonished by the scope of your mercy.

※ Before I was born, you knew I would resist your ways and challenge your authority, yet you gave me life *anyway.*
※ When I was unable to grasp my need and your provision for my soul, you drew me to Jesus *anyway.*
※ When I am in denial or clueless to deal with lingering sin and long-held, merciless attitudes, you continue to show mercy *anyway*—working to shape me more and more into the likeness of Christ.

I am grateful that you do not leave me on my own to find my way through life. You are my Guide, my Refuge, my Rescuer, and my Comforter. I encounter the challenges of this day with anticipation, knowing that your mercy surrounds me, and your love never fails.

Thank you for granting me a steadfast spirit
and sending me out in your name as a reconciling force
with mercy that overflows freely and wisely from a grateful heart.

In the name of Jesus, I pray. Amen.

Miracles

*Then Job answered the LORD and said: "I know that you can
do all things, and that no purpose of yours can be thwarted."*
Job 42:1–2

*"But I want you to know that the Son of Man has authority
on earth to forgive sins." So he said to the paralyzed
man, "Get up, take your mat and go home."*
Matthew 9:6

*The angel said to the women, "Do not be afraid, for I
know that you are looking for Jesus, who was crucified.
He is not here; he has risen, just as he said."*
Matthew 28:5–6

All-Powerful God,

You are the Holy Ruler—the proactive and patient One who forms
and transforms your creation. You are the God of miracles. Today, I
gratefully submit to your complete authority over my life.

Lord Jesus, thank you for the miraculous exchange of my sin for
your holiness. I am grateful for the continual flow of the miraculous
into my life as I walk in your Presence in always-accessible love and
peace. In daily spiritual battles, you fight on my behalf—and no one
can remove me from your hand.

I praise you for the gift of faith and understanding to see your
miraculous work in things I take for granted. Thank you for designing

the earth as my home and bringing forth food for my sustenance. Thank you for preserving the truth of your existence, care, and power through thousands of years so that this generation could know you.

I am so grateful for the miracle of your Holy Spirit to counsel, direct, and reassure me of your constant vigilance. Thank you for welcoming me to share life with you today: I am cherished, kept, and dearly loved.

In view of your miracles—past and present—I thank you for inviting me to seek your counsel, your will, and your intervention. I know it is within your power to end any heartache and suffering and the events that cause them. Whether you reverse the laws of nature to bring relief or affirm your care with the greater miracle of your constant, sustaining Presence, I thank you that your "grace is sufficient" (2 Corinthians 12:9).

> Thank you for calling me to praise you in every season
> and to celebrate your miracles: the works that I witness
> and the far-reaching plans you are fulfilling,
> my good and loving God.

> In the name of Jesus, I pray. Amen.

Near

The Lord is near to all who call on him,
to all who call on him in truth.
Psalm 145:18

"Here I am!¹ I stand at the door and knock. If anyone
hears my voice and opens the door, I will come in
and eat with that person, and they with me."
Revelation 3:20

I have been crucified with Christ and I no
longer live, but Christ lives in me.
Galatians 2:20

Faithful Lord,

Thank you for the stunning declaration that you choose to be *with me.*
I am so grateful that I live in you and you in me: your Presence fills
and nourishes my soul. As I reflect on the nature of your nearness,
I am consumed by the sacred security of life with you. You are the
One who surrounds me—my God who sees and understands. You
are the One who is *here.*

I honor you today as my Commander and my life's mission. Nothing
surpasses the importance of nearness to you: "*Yes, everything else is*
worthless when compared with the priceless gain of knowing Christ
Jesus my Lord" (Philippians 3:8 TLB).

---

¹ Jesus Christ, see Revelation 1:1–2

My devoted God, I love you because you first loved me and planned for me to be yours—to share life with you—before the creation of the world. Thank you for the ability to remain attentive to your Spirit as we travel through this day together. Thank you for inflaming my heart as you reveal fresh meaning in scripture, strengthening my soul.

Thank you for your constant call to commune with you. What peace, discernment, and God-control flow from your reminder to cover every person and every decision in prayer!

Thank you for reminding me of my most important task today: to be focused on your Spirit. Out of the abundance of your soul-fueling Presence I can pour lovingkindness into my surroundings—and the world will understand who you are, my ever-present God.

Holy One, you are set apart in perfection
but as near as my next heartbeat.
Because you are intensely interested and profoundly working,
I trust your purposes and find my deepest fulfillment in your
company. Thank you for carrying me close to your heart.

In the name of Jesus, I pray. Amen.

New Creation

Therefore, if anyone is in Christ, the new creation
has come: The old has gone, the new is here!
2 Corinthians 5:17

"Forget the former things;
do not dwell on the past.
See, I am doing a new thing!
Now it springs up; do you not perceive it?
I am making a way in the wilderness
and streams in the wasteland."
Isaiah 43:18

God Who Works Wonders,

I am in awe of you because you never change—but your Presence changes everything. Thank you for bringing a fresh sense of your faithfulness today.

I praise you for making me new: actually and permanently new. Thank you for bringing me to the point of surrender, burying the old life, and awakening me to the vivid future of life within your light.

As you melt and remake the core of my being, I am surprised at the depth of your transforming work. Thank you for steadily molding me to think and react in love like Christ. I am so grateful for new experiences of your firm commitment and your power at work in real life as you bring forth...

❋ righteousness from my heart's rebellion (Titus 3:4–7).
❋ compassion from callousness (Ephesians 4:32).
❋ clarity from confusion (Psalm 119:169).
❋ new direction from distress or disappointment (Proverbs 3:5–6).

Thank you for the patience you demonstrate as you tenderly care for me. When I pause to let this sink into my consciousness, I experience the outpouring of hope—deep confidence—you always intended for me.

❋ There is no heart too hard for you to change.
❋ There is no ruin you cannot rebuild.
❋ There is no shame you cannot redeem for good.

Thank you for wrapping me in radiant praise instead of a spirit of defeat.

Thank you for pouring your Shalom—soul wellness—into
my being and giving me a heart eager to live a life worthy of my
purpose: to know you and love you with all my heart, soul, and
strength.

In the name of Jesus, I pray. Amen.

Open

When he[2] was at the table with them, he took bread,
gave thanks, broke it and began to give it to them. Then
their eyes were opened and they recognized him, and
he disappeared from their sight. They asked each other,
"Were not our hearts burning within us while he talked
with us on the road and opened the Scriptures to us?"
Luke 24:30–32

You open your hand and satisfy the desires of every living thing.
The LORD is righteous in all his ways and faithful in all he does.
Psalm 145:16–17

Ever-Present God,

I honor you as the All-Knowing One who opened the days of history: the same One who walks ahead of me into this day (Genesis 1:1; Psalm 23:3–4). Thank you for throwing open the floodgates of your power and love to carve the way to you through Jesus, "the way and the truth and the life" (John 14:6).

I am overwhelmed by the openness, freedom, and companionship we share—oneness. I am grateful for the courage to be real in your Presence, knowing that every conversation is bathed in love and understanding. Thank you for welcoming me to lay open my ongoing struggles of body and mind as first steps in gaining wisdom and healing.

---

[2] Jesus Christ, see Luke 24:13–16; 33–35.

I praise you for deeply connecting my soul to scripture, stirring my intellect and emotions with the assurance of your word. Thank you for reminding me that, throughout time, you have intentionally stepped into humanity's chaos and brought peace, wisdom, and provision (Psalm 77:10–12). You have promised revival and renewal (Acts 3:19; Colossians 3:10). You are drawing me into wholeness (Romans 8:6). You are building a habit of gratitude in me (Psalm 147:1).

Thank you for opening my soul to see beyond my analytical mind and embrace the radical life of faith you have ordained for me. My joy and security come as I walk not in full knowledge of the path ahead but in the light of your Presence. Thank you for revealing today's priority: to be in open, intentional communication with you so that my first response is to rush to you in distress or praise you for success. As I commune with you, my love for you expands and spills into love for those around me—and obstacles become opportunities to pray.

Thank you for opening my heart to embrace your Presence
and to adore you, my wise, loving, and trustworthy God.
I look forward, eagerly, to the day when you will welcome me
with open arms into heaven where I will see your face.

In the name of Jesus, I pray. Amen.

Opposition

*As for me, I call to God, and the LORD saves me. Evening,
morning and noon I cry out in distress, and he hears
my voice. He rescues me unharmed from the battle
waged against me, even though many oppose me.*
Psalm 55:16–18

*For the joy set before him he endured the cross, scorning
its shame, and sat down at the right hand of the throne
of God. Consider him who endured such opposition from
sinners, so that you will not grow weary and lose heart.*
Hebrews 12:2–3

God Who Makes a Way,

Thank you for summoning me into holiness when conflict swirls around me—calling me apart to be pure and honorable in the presence of those who oppose me. Thank you for revealing that you alone fully perceive every motive and every response to conflict. You are the invincible One: I praise you for accomplishing justice tempered with mercy and for offering to guide every action with unmatched insight and love.

Today, I thank you for reminding me to keep my eyes on you, Jesus, the One who endured the suffering and shame of the cross for the joy of bringing me new life. Thank you for showing me that "all the treasures of wisdom and knowledge" are found in you (Colossians

2:2–3). I am not alone in challenges or tough decisions. I do not have to—and should not—try to control everything.

I praise you for your power over the spiritual forces of evil that seek to undermine your purposes and my faithfulness. Although Satan accuses me night and day, you uplift, renew, and strengthen me so that I can stand my ground for good even in the face of unjust criticism and hate (Ephesians 6:14; Revelation 12:10).

Thank you for reminding me that my role is not to recreate those around me—you alone can change hearts—but to speak the truth in love. Knowing that your Holy Spirit is my gracious guard, I thank you for releasing me from the burden of other people's opinions and the fear that my words will be inadequate or twisted into something other than the good I desire.

Thank you for the assurance that you are working, even now,
to achieve lasting results for those who love you.
Because I live by your power and goodness today,
I am more than a conqueror (Romans 8:37).

I praise you and pray in the name of Jesus. Amen.

Overcome

*You, dear children, are from God and have
overcome them, because the one who is in you is
greater than the one who is in the world.*
1 John 4:4

Do not be overcome by evil, but overcome evil with good.
Romans 12:21

*I have told you these things, so that in me you may
have peace. In this world you will have trouble.
But take heart! I have overcome the world.*
John 16:33

My Eternal Protector and Provider,

Thank you for drawing me into a God-centered perspective today: "Our help is in the name of the LORD, the Maker of heaven and earth" (Psalm 124:8). All-Powerful God, thank you for being my refuge, my safe place, and my defense in times of trouble. There is no obstacle that can defeat, deflect, or delay your powerful work. You are the overcoming One.

I honor you today as *God-with-Us* and also *God-for-Us*. When circumstances—actual or anticipated—shatter my serenity, I am grateful to see you rebuke the turbulence around me and calm the storm inside me. Because you truly, deeply care about my well-being, you wrap your protective love around me like a wall of fire.

When I feel overwhelmed, I am thankful that my prayer doesn't go into thin air but into your heart. As I lay my requests before you, I wait—expectantly.

Thank you for showing me "the wonders of your great love" (Psalm 17:7). Throughout history, we see your power to win battles, move nature, and overcome death itself in the promise of resurrection and life with you forever. Even the gates of hell will not prevail against your people.

With you, nothing is impossible. Nothing. No circumstance or conflict is beyond the reach of your understanding or ability to intervene. And, knowing that your ways are higher and more far-reaching than mine, I thank you today for inviting me to release worry and embrace your care.

> I praise you because you alone are everlasting.
> Your power is absolute. Your love for me is complete.
> And I am so grateful to be—yours.
>
> In the name of Jesus, I pray. Amen.

Patience

The Lord is not slow in keeping his promise, as some understand slowness. Instead, he is patient with you, not wanting anyone to perish, but everyone to come to repentance.
2 Peter 3:9

As a prisoner for the Lord, then, I urge you to live a life worthy of the calling you have received. Be completely humble and gentle; be patient, bearing with one another in love.
Ephesians 4:1–2

Being confident of this, that he who began a good work in you will carry it on to completion until the day of Christ Jesus.
Philippians 1:6

Compassionate God,

How enduringly, resolutely patient you are! You are the infinite, unchanging, only God—unique in perspective and authority. As you work out your plans with a complete understanding of humanity—all time, all people, and all events—I am astounded by your patience and assured by your promises. *Your word never fails* (Luke 1:37).

Before creation, you planned to faithfully love me, watch over me, and bless me with heartfelt patience. As I inhale the calmness of your Presence, I am able to surrender my stress into your Almighty care. Thank you for instilling a habit of trusting obedience, so that I can grow like a well-nourished "tree planted by streams of water, which yields its fruit in season" (Psalm 1:3).

Lord Jesus, as we walk through this day, I am grateful for your perfect life example. I praise you for focusing firmly on your life goal: to rescue and renew me (Jude 1:24). Thank you for patiently enduring betrayal, false accusations, abuse, and even the cross for the joy of our future together. Thank you for investing your time in me—for unfailing love and persistence.

As you unfold your plans to accomplish righteousness in my surroundings, I thank you for teaching me that "love is patient," and you are Love (1 Corinthians 13:4; 1 John 4:8). I am grateful today for your work to produce divine patience in me so that I am not easily offended or angered—and able to forgive wholeheartedly and often (Colossians 3:12–14).

Thank you for planting patience and cultivating composure in me. I praise you for the work of your Spirit to remind me of your truth:
You are constantly redeeming and re-creating.
You are working in and through all things.
And there is more blessing
than I have imagined—in your patience.

Thank you. In the name of Jesus, I pray. Amen.

Peace

You will keep in perfect peace those whose minds
are steadfast, because they trust in you.
Isaiah 26:3

But the wisdom that comes from heaven is first of all
pure; then peace-loving, considerate, submissive, full of
mercy and good fruit, impartial and sincere. Peacemakers
who sow in peace reap a harvest of righteousness.
James 3:17–18

God of Perfect Peace,

I praise you for the indescribable assurance of your Spirit—the source of peace that permeates my soul, brings wisdom to my mind, and infuses my relationships with thoughtfulness.

I praise you because your peace is more than the absence of conflict, peril, or confusion. It is a covenant of life and wholeness.

As I stand here in your favor, I praise you for peace that *rules* my heart. Thank you for showing me that peace is a gift not to be received dispassionately but pursued and nurtured: "the mind governed by the Spirit is life and peace" (Romans 8:6).

Thank you for imprinting moments of sacred understanding on my mind—events in which your absolute power is revealed. As I *speak your name in praise* and remember that you are constantly watching over me, peace fills my soul and even impacts people and events around me. Thank you for allowing me to see evil confounded, malice thwarted, and darkness flee. Thank you for faith strengthened and joy restored.

I praise you for sending me into this day as a peacemaker in your name and in your power. I am eternally grateful...

❈ for the invitation to trust you, the One who can dismiss dangerous storms and chaos with a command: *"Peace, be still!"* (Mark 4:39 NKJV).

❈ for deep tranquility that *exceeds my comprehension,* knowing that you hold me forever (Philippians 4:7).

❈ for deep, lasting peace that is always available as I turn to you in grateful trust (John 14:24).

As I walk with you today,
I thank you for abundant peace
that overflows from the shared celebration of life
on your path—and in your eternal care (Romans 15:13).

In the name of Jesus, I pray. Amen.

Perseverance

*Therefore, since we are surrounded by such a great cloud
of witnesses, let us throw off everything that hinders
and the sin that so easily entangles. And let us run with
perseverance the race marked out for us, fixing our
eyes on Jesus, the pioneer and perfecter of faith.*
Hebrews 12:1–2

*And let us not grow weary while doing good, for in
due season we shall reap if we do not lose heart.*
Galatians 6:9

My Steadfast God,

You are relentlessly faithful. Thank you for drawing me into your
energizing Presence. Time with you refreshes and fortifies my spirit
beyond my own ability and strength. Thank you for lifting me up
and leading me on with trust that you remain firm in your resolve
and perfect in your power.

I praise you for reminding me that you are infinitely able to guide me
through any circumstance or condition—even long-term struggles.
Thank you for revealing that my own example of faithfulness can be
most potent in difficult times: my reactions are a priceless testimony
and guide to those around me who are *always* observing my life.

Lord Jesus, I am in awe of your constant commitment to me. When
I think of your determination to make your way toward the cross,
knowing you would die for me there, I am overwhelmed with love

and gratitude. Only through faith can I begin to comprehend the nature of the ongoing challenge—the spiritual battle underway for my faithfulness and fruitfulness—and the scope of your intervention.

- ❋ There is nothing that can separate me from your persevering love.
- ❋ The priorities and pursuits of the past—even my sin-drenched self-absorption and carelessness—do not prevent me from following you wholeheartedly now.
- ❋ There is no obstacle too great nor any sacrifice too personal to unravel the work you are accomplishing in me and through me.

As I see rivers you have carved through valleys, I begin to comprehend your power to make a way for "impossible" things to happen.

I am so grateful that the same divine power
that raised Christ from the dead is at work in me
to accomplish your plans through everything
I encounter as we walk together today.

I pray and praise you in the name of Jesus. Amen.

Pleasure

God of Gladness,

As I soak in your Presence, you pour joy into my soul, and I embrace the day with divine anticipation. You are the Source of my deepest pleasure, my Bread of Life, and the author of my contentment. Thank you for teaching me to trust you above all else. As you shape my understanding of you, the True and Living God, my attitude toward life shifts, and I find deep pleasure in the things you value.

- ※ Thank you for joy as I surrender to your will rather than rely on my own strength, knowing you will provide everything I need for all you call me to do (Psalm 147:10–11).
- ※ I am grateful for the gladness you bring as I join you in replacing injustice and hate with fairness and kindness (Isaiah 1:11–19).

⁂ Thank you for humility to confess my wrongdoing—my mistakes and my intentional sin—knowing that refreshing times follow repentance (Acts 3:19).

Thank you for commanding me to prioritize time and resources for the treasure of your company. Thank you for showering me with lavish grace, reconciliation, and the sheer joy of your Presence. You are pleased when I pray and delighted with my desire to follow you (Ephesians 1:7–10).

I praise you for the joy of giving grace to others as you have given mercy and goodwill to me (Luke 6:35–36). I am grateful today for increasing faith to embrace your word and celebrate your purposes (Hebrews 10:38).

Thank you for using the rollercoaster of life to draw me closer
and remind me that my life is built on you:
profound and lasting joy
is not based on my condition
but on your character.

All else fades in the pleasure of your loving company,
the One who "who richly provides us with everything
for our enjoyment" (1 Timothy 6:17).

In the name of Jesus, I praise and thank you. Amen.

Power

Who is like you—majestic in holiness,
awesome in glory,
working wonders?
Exodus 15:11

"Yours, LORD, is the greatness and the power
and the glory and the majesty and the splendor,
for everything in heaven and earth is yours.
Yours, LORD, is the kingdom;
you are exalted as head over all."
1 Chronicles 29:11

May the God of hope fill you with all joy and peace
as you trust in him, so that you may overflow
with hope by the power of the Holy Spirit.
Romans 15:13

Almighty God,

I honor you today as the Creator and Commander of the Universe: the eternally vigilant and intervening God. You are my Deliverer, my Fortress, and my soul's hiding place. Thank you for reminding me daily that I am formed, nourished, and secured by you, my loving God.

All-Powerful One, throughout history you have moved heaven and earth on behalf of your people.

❊　By your power, you held back the waters of the Red Sea to accomplish safe passage then released a flood to defeat your enemies (Exodus 14:21–27).

❊　By your authority, you have healed, raised the dead, and cast out destructive demonic forces (Matthew 8:16; Luke 7:14–15).

❊　By your love, you took hold of me, sacrificed yourself for my sin, and accomplished eternal justice—with mercy—to bring me to you (1 Peter 3:18).

As you enforce your will, you will ultimately destroy every influence that denies you, deceives us, and embraces evil—placing every harmful, painful trauma and disaster under your dominion. Even death will be under your feet.

Holy God, thank you for your promise to accomplish good and bring honor to your name as we walk together. I am most at peace, most inspired, and most joy-filled when I consciously consider your powerful Presence.

Filled with your Spirit and attentive to your will,
I praise you for your strength at work in me to accomplish
"immeasurably more than all we ask or imagine" (Ephesians 3:20).

In the name of Jesus, I pray. Amen.

Questions

"Call to me and I will answer you and tell you great
and unsearchable things you do not know."
Jeremiah 33:3

For they received the message with great eagerness and
examined the Scriptures every day to see if what Paul said
was true. As a result, many of them believed, as did also a
number of prominent Greek women and many Greek men.
Acts 17:11–12

You will seek me and find me when you seek me with all your heart.
Jeremiah 29:13

God, My Wise Teacher,

I honor you today as the Dayspring of knowledge and insight: you are the Truth and the Giver of Enlightenment. Thank you for creating in me a mind that instinctively searches for what is real and right. Looking through the perspective of your holiness, power, and love, I can see what is valid and good.

Thank you for inviting me to seek knowledge and answers from you and assuring me that my prayers are valued. Your Spirit draws my searching mind into understanding beyond my human reach—things only unfolded in your Presence.

Lord, my Anchor and my Shield, thank you for dispelling distortions that swirl around me. I am grateful that your love and your grace are vast enough to handle my questions.

❇ **When I encounter evil**, thank you for assurance that you face it with me. Lord Jesus, I am grateful that your plan to eliminate evil is already underway and will be completed when you return in victory (1 Corinthians 15:20–26).

❇ **When I experience loss, rejection, or illness**, thank you for drawing me close and building my faith—whether your answer is yes, no, or wait. Thank you for teaching me that understanding "why" is not as comforting as being embraced by your Presence (Psalm 34:18).

❇ **When I need direction**, thank you for answers in your scripture and through the prompting of your Spirit (Psalm 119:105; John 16:13).

My Guide and Encourager,
thank you for motivating my questions
so that I run to you for answers.
As my faith and insight grows, I praise you
for speaking hope, direction, and life to my grateful soul.

In the name of Jesus, I pray. Amen.

Quiet

"The LORD your God in your midst,
The Mighty One, will save;
He will rejoice over you with gladness,
He will quiet you with His love,
He will rejoice over you with singing."
Zephaniah 3:17 (NKJV)

He got up, rebuked the wind and said to the waves,
"Quiet! Be still!" Then the wind died down and it
was completely calm. He said to his disciples, "Why
are you so afraid? Do you still have no faith?"
Mark 4:39–40

God Over All,

Thank you for drawing me into quietness: the priceless, sacred serenity of your Presence. As you summon me into silence, I become intensely aware of your loving attention to my life. Thank you for inviting me to be quiet and simply inhale the reality that you are my God—constantly watching and whispering to my soul.

In the grateful quietness, your Presence radiates assurance. Complaints and concerns fall silent as I meditate on your character: you are genuinely gracious, merciful, faithful, and full of lovingkindness (Exodus 34:6). I am grateful to find my identity—and answers—in recounting the nature of my God.

As stress fades into worship, I become acutely aware of the call to honor you above all else. Your flawless, compassionate character is worthy of my complete attention, respect, and adoration. I am so thankful to find that you are in this moment—*in this life with me.*

You are my strong foundation. Because you are within me, I will not fear, fall, or fail to accomplish the purpose you intend for me. In time alone with you, I praise you for igniting good things in my heart and providing the inspiration to follow your lead. Thank you for confidence that the work you have assigned to me will never be in vain but will produce results beyond my comprehension.

Thank you, Lord, for not shouting at my soul, hoping to be heard over the demands of the day. Thank you for inviting me to come away and quietly commune with you—the love of my life.

As I sit in silence before you, Almighty God,
I am grateful to hear the secrets of your wisdom and your will.

I am eternally grateful to you, Lord—for calling me into quietness.

In the name of Jesus, I pray and praise you. Amen.

Raise

*For what I received I passed on to you as of first
importance: that Christ died for our sins according to
the Scriptures, that he was buried, that he was raised
on the third day according to the Scriptures.*
1 Corinthians 15:3–4

*Since, then, you have been raised with Christ, set your hearts on
things above, where Christ is, seated at the right hand of God.*
Colossians 3:1

Eternally Living God,

I honor you as the One who declares the end from the beginning
(Isaiah 46:10). What you have started, you will finish. As you gaze
on humanity, you see a harvest of hope: you are raising up a righteous
family for yourself to live in love and peace (Matthew 9:35–38).
Thank you for reminding me not to dwell on—or become immersed
in—the evil in the world but to raise my eyes to you.

Lord Jesus, I honor you today as the risen Christ: the One who is
living, working, and returning to make all things perfect. Thank you
for loving me enough to face the cross for me. How enormous was
your sacrifice on my behalf!

- ※ You carried my sin *with you* to the cross: destroying it,
  burying it, and wiping away any judgment against me.
- ※ When you died, my sin died with you. When you rose from
  the grave, I also received the promise of life after death.

✳ And now, freed from the destructive grip of sin, you raise me up to a fresh start, a new path.

Thank you for raising me up *for yourself*: I am chosen and greatly valued (Ephesians 1:4–5). You have given me a purpose. I am a dwelling place of Christ and a channel of blessing to those around me (Galatians 2:20; Ephesians 2:10).

Thank you for lifting me up and setting me on solid ground—
I greet this day anchored in your hope and authority.
As a vine draws nourishment from a sturdy branch,
your Life flows into me so that your Spirit's courage
and kindness feed the culture around me.

As I rise to meet the challenges of this season,
I am grateful to be secured in you,
propelled by you, equipped by you,
and filled with you—the risen Christ.

In your name, Lord Jesus, I pray and praise. Amen.

Rebellion

Who is wise? Let them realize these things.
Who is discerning? Let them understand.
The ways of the LORD are right;
the righteous walk in them,
but the rebellious stumble in them.
Hosea 14:9

Many times he delivered them, but they were bent on rebellion
and they wasted away in their sin. Yet he took note of their
distress when he heard their cry; for their sake he remembered
his covenant and out of his great love he relented.
Psalm 106:43–45

My God Who Saves,

I honor you as my faultless, forgiving God. You are the All-Powerful, Perfect One. With a breath, you could consume those who rebel against your good commands:

> *"Who would not fear You, O King of the nations? For*
> *this is Your rightful due."* (Jeremiah 10:7 NKJV)

But in lovingkindness, you choose to save and welcome us:

> *"There is no fear in love. But perfect love drives out fear,*
> *because fear has to do with punishment."* (1 John 4:18)

Lord Jesus, in respect and awe-struck gratitude, I praise you for sacrificing yourself for me. **You have exchanged my rebellion for your righteousness**.

I praise you today as the One who rescues me from the deception and destruction of sin, even when I have ignored you, excused myself, or been too spiritually blind to avoid Satan's traps. Thank you for applying redemptive mercy so complete that it purifies my thinking and changes my worldview.

Thank you for the continuing intervention of your Spirit—like a refining fire that works to melt away everything unholy and leaves only the life-altering desire to please you (Malachi 2:17–3:3).

Thank you for your patience with this world—for time and tenderness to draw more people to yourself. Thank you for persistently and lovingly moving me to you in genuine, full restoration.

Because you want me to be in your holy Presence,
experiencing your strength and wholeness,
you turn my darkness into light
and my rebellion into eager obedience—
accomplishing things otherwise impossible.

Thank you, my Loving and Faithful God.
In Jesus' name, amen.

Receive

*In a loud voice they were saying: "Worthy is the Lamb,[3]
who was slain, to receive power and wealth and wisdom
and strength and honor and glory and praise!"*
Revelation 5:12

*Yet to all who did receive him, to those who believed in his
name, he gave the right to become children of God.*
John 1:12

*Let us then approach God's throne of grace with
confidence, so that we may receive mercy and
find grace to help us in our time of need.*
Hebrews 4:16

My Gracious God,

Far more than anyone else in heaven or earth, you deserve to receive
my praise, trust, and steadfast love. I honor you today as my Designer,
my Savior, and my Sustainer. You are the Holy and Dependable One.
By your will, I exist. In your care, I thrive.

I praise you for inviting me to receive "the life that is truly life"
(1 Timothy 6:19). Only you could open my mind and heart to
embrace this gift of harmony with you, the Creator of the universe.
Thank you for teaching me that this gift—freely given and freely

---

[3] "John saw Jesus coming toward him and said, 'Look, the Lamb of God, who
takes away the sin of the world!'" (John 1:29).

received—requires the willing surrender of my life to your loving, higher purposes. Thank you for the gladness we share in our mutual devotion: I love you because you first loved me (1 John 4:19).

As I echo the joy that flows from your heart, I praise you for pouring yourself into my soul and building your qualities into my life.

- ❈ Thank you for love so complete and powerful that it overwhelms evil and inspires my commitment to give as I have received (John 3:16; Romans 12:21).
- ❈ Thank you for a profound testimony of praise that erupts from peace and joy beyond my understanding (Philippians 4:6–7; Acts 16:25–34).
- ❈ Thank you for patience and faithfulness: never giving up on me and leading me to intercede today for those who need to receive your saving, healing touch (Ephesians 4:2; Hebrews 10:23).

I am so grateful to receive divine strength for everything I need today (1 Peter 1:3). Thank you for moment-by-moment grace so that you are honored in my life and—through the work of your Spirit— the people in my path receive a taste of your blessings.

In the name of Jesus, I pray. Amen.

Reconcile

And since, when we were his enemies,
we were brought back to God by the death of his Son,
what blessings he must have for us
now that we are his friends
and he is living within us!
Romans 5:10 (TLB)

Be kind and compassionate to one another,
forgiving each other,
just as in Christ God forgave you.
Ephesians 4:32

God Who Welcomes Me,

Your self-sacrificing mercy is simply beyond my comprehension.
Thank you for reconciling the wrecked God-to-human relationship
and restoring the broken peace: a mission accomplished only through
deep love, tender grace, and profound patience *for me.*

Lord Jesus, your deepest crisis—your battle for my soul—achieved
your greatest victory:

- ※ My transgressions became your trauma (Mark 14:32–36; 1
  Peter 3:18).
- ※ My punishment became your cross to bear (1 Peter 2:24).
- ※ Your peace became my peace (John 14:27).

I honor you as the One who brings deep healing to my soul. Thank you for warning me that I will face troubled relationships in this world—divisiveness that cuts like a sword. But in conflict with those who reject me, embrace spiritual death, or see your sacrifice as senseless, I thank you that your heart weeps with mine and your Spirit provides a pathway.

Thank you for leading me to confess and seek reconciliation where I have wronged those around me, whether intentionally or carelessly. Thank you for love and strength to forgive those who have harmed me whether or not they seek my forgiveness. Most of all, thank you for reconciling my relationship with you—a one-sided act of mercy.

As I stand in your favor and love,
genuinely welcomed into your Presence,
I thank you for drawing me to yourself
and sending me out with a sacred assignment
to spread hope and healing.
Thank you for the grace and the gift of reconciliation.

In the name of Jesus, I pray. Amen.

Rejoice

Rejoice always, pray continually, give thanks in all circumstances; for this is God's will for you in Christ Jesus.
1 Thessalonians 5:16–18

Then I heard what sounded like a great multitude, like the roar of rushing waters and like loud peals of thunder, shouting: "Hallelujah! For our Lord God Almighty reigns. Let us rejoice and be glad and give him glory! For the wedding of the Lamb has come, and his bride has made herself ready."[4]
Revelation 19:6

My Good and Loving God,

Joy radiates from your Presence: when I turn my attention to you, the light of your face filters into my heart, and I rejoice over you my God, my Guide, and the delight of my life. Thank you for a gift of rejoicing that reaches beyond the temporary idols of human circumstance or the fickle opinions of other people—an ability to rejoice that even transcends human suffering.

I praise you for revealing that there is a permanence in spiritual rejoicing: a foundation of joy planted deeply within the souls of all who believe in you (Galatians 5:22). In your Presence, there is joy that is rich, loving, and secure. *I rejoice because you are with me.*

---

[4] The "Lamb" is Jesus Christ, and the "bride" is his church composed of all believers.

141

❋ I have been rescued from the grip of Satan and I belong to you, the God of the universe (1 Corinthians 6:19–20).

❋ I have been chosen by you and adopted as your child (Ephesians 1:3–8).

❋ I have been forgiven of all my sins and my name is written in heaven (Colossians 1:13–14; Luke 10:20).

❋ You "delight to show mercy" (Micah 7:18), and there is a celebration in heaven over my repentance and renewed heart (Luke 15:7).

I praise you for giving me new life, so that I am "filled with an inexpressible and glorious joy, for you are receiving the end result of your faith, the salvation of your souls" (1 Peter 1:8).

> Thank you for drawing me into a habit of rejoicing
> so that good thoughts are stored in my heart,
> and my soul continually feasts on the reality
> of your goodness, faithfulness, and enduring love.

> In the name of Jesus, I pray. Amen.

Remain

He is the Maker of heaven and earth, the sea, and
everything in them—he remains faithful forever.
Psalm 146:6

"Remain in me, as I also remain in you. No branch can
bear fruit by itself; it must remain in the vine. Neither
can you bear fruit unless you remain in me."
John 15:4

"Here I am! I stand at the door and knock. If anyone
hears my voice and opens the door, I will come in
and eat with that person, and they with me."
Revelation 3:20

My Steadfast God,

You are my Constant One: my peace and wholeness. When everything else changes, you remain *in* me and *for* me. You are my dwelling place.

Thank you for reminding me today that nothing is more valuable than walking with you. As I surrender to your leadership and commit to "keep my eyes always on the LORD" (Psalm 16:8), I thank you for replacing my performance-driven thinking and my soul-exhausting pride with your life-giving Light.

Thank you for inviting me to lay the events of this day at your feet and exchange worry for worship. Humbly, I acknowledge that your wisdom and foresight are far beyond my intellectual grasp. As you weave your peace into my soul, I perceive beauty in the journey and a heavy spirit melting into a heart full of praise (Isaiah 61:3).

Thank you for prompting me to remain in constant awareness of you today. You are God over my busiest hours and my rest. As my spirit communes with your Spirit, I am grateful to experience an outpouring of soul nourishment: love, joy, and peace that overflow into my decisions and relationships. Thank you for being my loyal companion. You are my attentive friend who knows me deeply and loves me consistently.

Today, I am simply amazed at your faithfulness. Unlike drifting sand, you remain the unshakable Solid Rock—my secure footing today and into the eternal future. I am grateful to know that you are the ceaseless force for good in everything that exists in my life and the world you have created.

As I remain wholeheartedly committed
to you, I am surprised to see
the depth of holiness you bring into
ordinary spaces and encounters—
your Spirit's gift of wisdom and hope to those you bring into my
life. And I am grateful to walk through this day—with you.

In the name of Jesus, I pray. Amen.

Remember

Look to the LORD and his strength; seek his face
always. Remember the wonders he has done, his
miracles, and the judgments he pronounced.
Psalm 105:4–5

"I, even I, am he who blots out your transgressions, for
my own sake, and remembers your sins no more."
Isaiah 43:25

Only be careful, and watch yourselves closely so that you
do not forget the things your eyes have seen or let them
fade from your heart as long as you live. Teach them
to your children and to their children after them.
Deuteronomy 4:9

God Over All,

As I take time today to examine your creative force and redeeming love, I am overwhelmed by your worth and your power on my behalf. *"I stand in awe of your deeds, LORD"* (Habakkuk 3:2). Thank you for examples of timeless truth revealed in your intervention.

God of heaven and earth, thank you for reminding me that you are aware of our needs, and you highly value our prayers. When the prophet Elijah prayed for rain to stop, it did not rain until he asked God to end the drought (James 5:17).

Invincible God, thank you for reminding me that you work through obedience (John 14:15). At your command, Joshua led his troops to march around the enemy city of Jericho, and their defenses crumbled (Joshua 6:1–5).

Compassionate God, thank you for reminding me that faith as small as a tiny seed can move mountains. Jesus taught us to trust as he banished evil and healed a boy whose case seemed hopeless (Matthew 17:14–20)—and taught us to pray "Thy will be done" (Matthew 6:10).

Knowing that your thoughts and actions are more far-reaching than mine (Isaiah 55:9), I am confident to release my future into your care as I remember your commitment.

> ✳ The same mighty power that raised Jesus from the dead is working in me (Ephesians 1:18–21).
> ✳ Insight beyond my own ability is available from your Spirit who lives in me (James 1:5; Galatians 2:20).
> ✳ Your love is so vast and so enduring that we will never outlive it or fathom its depth (Ephesians 3:16–19).

Today, I am grateful to be filled with your strength and grounded in your faithfulness—remembering that this moment is ordained by you and filled with your Presence.

With my whole heart, I praise you in the name of Jesus. Amen.

Restore

The LORD is my shepherd;
I shall not want.
He makes me to lie down in green pastures;
He leads me beside the still waters.
He restores my soul;
He leads me in the paths of righteousness
For His name's sake.
Psalm 23:1–3 (NKJV)

Restore to me the joy of your salvation and
grant me a willing spirit, to sustain me.
Psalm 51:12

God Who Holds Me,

I am so grateful today for a new and vibrant vision of your care. You are my life's support and resting place, my source of strength and motivation, my Counselor and my Peace.

Thank you for **restoring my soul** to the closeness you have always desired for me. Far more than I value my own life, and more than I can comprehend, you consider my soul precious. Lord Jesus, I honor you as the One who sits at the right hand of our Father interceding *for me* (Hebrews 7:25; 1 John 2:1–2).

Thank you for **refreshing my soul** with new evidence of your goodness, power, and compassion. When I inevitably walk through the challenges and destruction of this fallen world, I am grateful to pour out my heart to you, my trustworthy One, and experience your healing peace. Thank you for reminding me *in this moment* that you are my Savior, Encourager, and lifelong ally.

I praise you for **reassuring my soul** with hope and a path for the future, knowing that you have charted the way. I am so grateful for a new level of faith, knowing more deeply that you are absolutely dependable and will supply all I need to follow you.

My Restoring God, I honor you with confidence that you will finish the good work you have begun in me (1 Thessalonians 5:23–24). You have built my life on *your* faithfulness: you are my Cornerstone, my Sustainer, and my Guide (Ephesians 2:19–22).

> Thank you for the reviving fountain of your Presence.
> I am grateful for new energy and insight
> as you restore my heart, mind, and soul
> through the constant flow of your loving Spirit.
>
> I praise you in the name of Jesus. Amen.

Return

"I will give them a heart to know me, that I am the
LORD. They will be my people, and I will be their God,
for they will return to me with all their heart."
Jeremiah 24:5

"If we live, we live for the Lord; and if we die, we die for
the Lord. So, whether we live or die, we belong to the Lord.
For this very reason, Christ died and returned to life so that
he might be the Lord of both the dead and the living."
Romans 14:8–9

My Welcoming God,

I am so grateful that *you are my God:* the Almighty One who
designed me and now receives me with pleasure. Throughout history,
you have voiced the love-filled, life-changing theme, *"Return to me"*
(Isaiah 44:22).

How purposefully and intensely you pursue me! I praise you for
drawing me into your salvation. On the days that I follow you
wholeheartedly and the moments I wander away, I praise you for
urging me to focus on the reality of your Presence: you are with me
always. Lord Jesus, thank you for the stunning evidence of your love
and commitment portrayed...

⁂ in your *life-giving return* from the grave (Romans 8:34).
⁂ in your *invitation to return*—drawing me to yourself as only
you can (John 6:44; Revelation 3:20).

✻ in your *return at the end of time* when you fulfill your promise to bring a new heaven and a new sin-free, pain-free earth (2 Peter 3:13).

Holy God, I praise you for not putting up with sin; it hurts my soul and wounds other people. Thank you for reminding me that choosing to ignore your Spirit means turning my back on wisdom, good choices, and soul health. Thank you for prompting me again and again to return to you in confession, to know full forgiveness, and to experience the plans you are unfolding with clear-eyed gratitude.

As my thoughts return to you in this moment, I am amazed at the height of joy and depth of peace you provide—a taste of the future you will bring when you conquer all evil and turn every face to you.

You are my hope, my life, and my eternity,
and in this sacred moment I celebrate your promise:
"'Yes, I am coming soon.'" (Revelation 22:20).

In your holy name, Lord Jesus, I pray and praise you. Amen.

Reveal

He reveals deep and hidden things;
he knows what lies in darkness,
and light dwells with him.
Daniel 2:22

For in the gospel the righteousness of God is revealed—a
righteousness that is by faith from first to last, just as
it is written: "The righteous will live by faith."
Romans 1:17

Nothing in all creation is hidden from God's sight.
Everything is uncovered and laid bare before the
eyes of him to whom we must give account.
Hebrews 4:13

Sovereign God,

I praise you today as the Ever-Present One with a unique perspective on your human creation and your magnificent purposes. You are the only One who knows, *"What no eye has seen, what no ear has heard, what no human mind has conceived—the things God has prepared for those who love him"* (1 Corinthians 2:9).

Thank you for unveiling your will by revealing your character. As I meditate on your priorities throughout history—justice, mercy, and love—your direction for me becomes increasingly clear and my desire for holiness becomes more earnest.

I am grateful that your Word is "living and active" in me (Hebrews 4:12 ESV). Thank you for revealing the true motivations of my inner thoughts and uncovering reclusive sin so that I can walk with integrity before you.

Revealer of Secrets, I want to know *everything* about you, this world, and the future you are planning for me. But I acknowledge that you are the only one who truly possesses all wisdom. So, in faith, I praise you for reserving some knowledge for yourself alone. Thank you for revealing that my limited insight and foresight are *blessings* that encourage me to draw closer to you and rely on your timing and faithfulness.

> Thank you for your invitation to come to you
> with all things—*to keep asking and seeking.*
> Thank you for welcoming me to the celebration
> at the end of time when your good work
> and the stunning brilliance of your Presence
> are fully and finally revealed.

In the name of Jesus, I pray. Amen.

Righteous

For the word of the LORD is right and true;
he is faithful in all he does.
The LORD loves righteousness and justice;
the earth is full of his unfailing love.
Psalm 33:4–5

Very rarely will anyone die for a righteous person,
though for a good person someone might possibly dare
to die. But God demonstrates his own love for us in this:
While we were still sinners, Christ died for us.
Romans 5:7–8

But if anyone obeys his word, love for God is truly made
complete in them. This is how we know we are in him:
Whoever claims to live in him must live as Jesus did.
1 John 2:5-6

My Faithful God,

As I meditate on your righteousness—the pure perfection revealed in your love, laws, and actions—I am in awe of *your excellence*. You are the Flawless One, the All-Seeing Judge, and the Loving Savior.

Thank you for pulling my (sometimes hesitant) mind onto the path of righteousness with increasing joy in becoming more like Christ. As your Spirit speaks unbiased truth to my soul, I praise you as the One who slices through my polished surface to understand my inmost self: my heart from which all actions flow. I am grateful that your

Spirit is never misled by blinding preconceptions, secret selfishness, or partial truth.

Thank you, Lord Jesus, for exchanging my sin for your righteousness. As you illuminate this day, any unresolved shadows of soul or covert pessimism begin to give way to a holy perspective of peace. Your life-giving Spirit has *"freed me from the vicious circle of sin and death"* (Romans 8:2 TLB). You are able, actually able, to deal with lingering corruption as I embrace a new reality: my allegiance now belongs to you. Sin is not my leader or my life.

> *"He has delivered us from the domain of darkness and*
> *transferred us to the kingdom of his beloved Son."*
> Colossians 1:13 ESV

Your righteousness is even more than the blessed absence of evil. As you relieve me of the burden of sin, you do not leave me empty or aimless but bring a new, abundant life.

Thank you for replenishing me today
with your soul-refreshing Spirit: the fountain of all that is
good, reliable, genuinely loving, and only found in you.

In the name of Jesus, I pray. Amen.

Satisfy

Because your love is better than life,
my lips will glorify you.
I will praise you as long as I live,
and in your name I will lift up my hands.
I will be fully satisfied as with the richest of foods;
with singing lips my mouth will praise you.
Psalm 63:3

And when he[5] sees all that is accomplished by the anguish
of his soul, he shall be satisfied; and because of what he has
experienced, my righteous Servant shall make many to be
counted righteous before God, for he shall bear all their sins.
Isaiah 53:11 (TLB)

God Who Fills My Soul,

You are my Living Water: the One who watches over me, strengthens, encourages, and inspires me. *Nothing satisfies like your Presence.*

I honor you, Lord Jesus, as the One with all authority (Matthew 28:18). I praise you for your life on earth: for fully understanding what it means to be human and satisfying my hunger for companionship, understanding, and sustenance. Thank you for creating me to walk in your company. No pursuit of money, success, or approval infuses me with the indescribable contentment and vibrant life that you provide.

---

[5] Jesus Christ, see Ephesians 1:3-10.

More importantly, I thank you for fundamentally shifting my perspective—teaching me to follow you because of *who you are* and *what you have done*, not just what you can do for me now. Thank you for claiming my very soul as your own, facing the cruelty of the cross for the satisfaction of presenting me faultless to our loving Father (Hebrews 12:2; Jude 1:24).

Thank you for drawing me close and keeping my eyes steadily on you so that the desires of *your* heart, Lord, overwhelm the misdirected cravings of my body and mind. I humbly thank you for *not* giving me the things that I pray for with wrong motivations, and instead, opening my soul to embrace your ways that ultimately, more deeply satisfy.

I am so grateful that your peace and wisdom
are always within my reach as I come to you in prayer.
Like a spring of refreshing water, you fill *"everything
in every way"* (Ephesians 1:22–23), and I am blessed to find
my greatest satisfaction in you.

In the name of Jesus, I pray. Amen.

Search

*"For this is what the Sovereign LORD says: I myself
will search for my sheep and look after them."*
Ezekiel 34:11

*Search me, God, and know my heart; test me and
know my anxious thoughts. See if there is any offensive
way in me, and lead me in the way everlasting.*
Psalm 139:23–24

*And without faith it is impossible to please God, because
anyone who comes to him must believe that he exists
and that he rewards those who earnestly seek him.*
Hebrews 11:6

My Ever-Present God,

Before creation, you knew my life and planned to plant in my heart
a desire for eternal truth and unbending love. These qualities are
only perfectly poured out in you. Thank you for patiently drawing
me until the knowledge of you took root in my mind and surrender
to you became my grateful soul's reality.

Nothing is hidden from your sight: no thoughts or actions in my past,
present, or future. Thank you for even using clouds of uncertainty
as a reminder to search for you—my Source of Life and unchanging
Foundation.

All-Knowing God, I am grateful for your wisdom as I search for responses to the persistent working of evil in the world. Thank you for guiding me into understanding: the solution to the heartbreak of sin is *your Presence.* You are the Light of the World. Darkness and light cannot coexist; when the fullness of your Light enters, darkness is destroyed.

So, as I lay my concerns at your throne, I thank you for reminding me that resolutions lie not in my complaints but in my prayers and committed response. Knowing that others are seeking answers only found in you, I thank you for the God-given ability to understand the times and to address hard situations with grace that points to you.

Thank you for lovingly probing and purifying my *own* heart. You understand the origins and recesses of my beliefs, thoughts, and dreams—my unvarnished desires and the untapped potential of my life.

I am so grateful for your promises:
when I search for you with all my heart, I will find you,
and when I draw near to you, you will draw near to me.

Thank you for making your home—now and forever—in my heart.

In the name of Jesus, I pray. Amen.

Secure

I keep my eyes always on the LORD.
With him at my right hand, I will not be shaken.
Therefore my heart is glad and my tongue rejoices;
my body also will rest secure.
Psalm 16:8–9

As for God, his way is perfect: The LORD's word is flawless;
he shields all who take refuge in him. For who is God besides
the LORD? And who is the Rock except our God? It is God
who arms me with strength and keeps my way secure.
Psalm 18:30–32

God Who Keeps Me,

You are the Righteous Ruler, my Maker and Savior: God Over All. *You declare the end from the beginning; your unchanging purposes endure* (Isaiah 46:10).

How eternally secure and gladly accepted I am! You have complete power to save or destroy and to set up kingdoms or remove them, and yet you choose to notice and nurture me.

I honor you for your loyalty and your kindness. Thank you for embracing me with faithful, all-consuming love: You have rescued me from the grip of the enemy of my soul. Even in the most trying situations, I cannot be shaken from your hand (John 10:29). Thank you for grace to act with honor in the face of hostility and guidance to find truth when faced with deceit.

Thank you for the gifts of faith and courage (Hebrews 10:38). When my path is lined with pain—rejection or conflict—I thank you for strength to sacrifice my immediate desires for the greater good you are accomplishing.

Lord of heaven and earth, in your absolute knowledge, you are intensely aware and involved in every spiritual, physical, and emotional struggle I experience this day. Thank you for your eternal plan *not* to remove me from all conflict but to *send* me to bring hope and relief into dry and desolate places as the power of your Spirit flows through my life.

Thank you for the invitation to approach you boldly for both mercy and strength: for surrounding me with favor like a shield (Psalm 5:12). I walk in confidence today, knowing that you chart the way before me and lay your hand of blessing on me (Psalm 139:5).

You are *my* way, truth, and life (John 14:6).
I am grateful to live in the knowledge that I am
always treasured by you and secure in you.

In the name of Jesus, I pray. Amen.

Sovereign

*Ah, Sovereign L<small>ORD</small>, you have made the heavens
and the earth by your great power and outstretched
arm. Nothing is too hard for you.*
Jeremiah 32:17

*Do you not know? Have you not heard? The L<small>ORD</small> is the
everlasting God, the Creator of the ends of the earth. He will not
grow tired or weary, and his understanding no one can fathom. He
gives strength to the weary and increases the power of the weak.*
Isaiah 40:28–29

Almighty God,

You exist eternally; your Presence spans infinite time and distance.
You are the Sovereign Lord and the immortal King: *"I am the first
and I am the last; apart from me there is no God"* (Isaiah 44:6).

Thank you for including me in your creative work—in your plans for
this world in this time in history. I am grateful that all the days of my
life are established by you before they come to be (Psalm 139:16).

I praise you as the One who works wonders: the Ever-Present
authority who directs my steps. Thank you for intervening with
visible victories and for insight to celebrate your actions. I also
honor you for working in ways I cannot see. When my earthly
foundations—people and provisions—slip away, I thank you for
reminding me that you are my Fortress and Steadfast God. I praise

you for reorienting my heart to you in profoundly deeper faith and love.

I am so grateful for your continuing work to bring cleansing and wholeness in this world. Even generations of sin's influence cannot stand as you remake my inner nature and reveal a new way of living—aware of your sovereign embrace.

- ✳ You are the reliable, unwavering One: You are rock-solid and worthy of complete trust (Psalm 31:1–3).
- ✳ You are the Supreme Authority: Your purposes are permanent (Job 42:2).
- ✳ You are faithful and true to me (Deuteronomy 7:9; 1 Corinthians 1:8–9).

Lord Jesus, as I consider your complete authority over all things in heaven and on earth, I honor you as my Sovereign forever.
I am so grateful that your loving word stands eternally, and your favor greets me every new morning (Lamentations 3:22–23).

In your holy name I praise you, amen.

Speak

Many, LORD my God,
are the wonders you have done,
the things you planned for us.
None can compare with you;
were I to speak and tell of your deeds,
they would be too many to declare.
Psalm 40:5

The woman said, "I know that Messiah" (called Christ)
"is coming. When he comes, he will explain everything to us."
Then Jesus declared, "I, the one speaking to you—I am he."
John 4:25–26

My Living God,

Thank you for filling the universe and my soul with the power of your words and wisdom. I am grateful to know you as the One who sees me (Genesis 16:13), hears me (Exodus 3:7; 1 Peter 3:12), and speaks hope and understanding (Genesis 15:1–6; James 1:5). Thank you for communicating your power through your creation: "the skies proclaim the work of his hands" (Psalm 19:1).

- ❊ You spoke all things into existence (Genesis 1:3–27).
- ❊ You sustain everything by your word (Hebrews 1:3).
- ❊ You outlined laws for living (Exodus 20:1–17) and taught us to love you and each other as you love us (John 13:34).

✳ You spoke the eternal promises, *"I am going there to prepare a place for you"*[6] (John 14:2) and *"I am with you always"* (Matthew 28:19–20).

Thank you for faith-encouraging answers and faith-testing interludes. Even in a dark night of the soul when I don't *feel* your Presence or hear deeply desired answers, I am grateful that your sacred silence leads me to self-examination, confession, and trusting praise.

You are my Companion and my life's Guide. So, when you call me to tasks beyond my power and expertise—the work that only you can accomplish—I am grateful to remember your promise to provide Holy Spirit-filled words and wisdom.

As we walk through this day together,
I thank you for speaking your eternal blessing over me:
to graciously make your face shine on me and
fill my heart with your peace (Numbers 6:24–26).

In the name of Jesus, I pray. Amen.

---

[6] The Father's house, i.e., God's Presence in heaven

Stand

But the plans of the LORD *stand firm forever,*
the purposes of his heart through all generations.
Psalm 33:11

Now it is God who makes both us and you stand firm in Christ.
He anointed us, set his seal of ownership on us, and put his
Spirit in our hearts as a deposit, guaranteeing what is to come.
2 Corinthians 1:21–22

For the Spirit God gave us does not make us timid,
but gives us power, love and self-discipline.
2 Timothy 1:7

God My Strength,

I simply stand in awe of you: In this very moment, you are my Solid Rock, my Safe Harbor, and my Flawless Leader. I am grateful to rely on your words: *"'My purpose will stand, and I will do all that I please.'"* (Isaiah 46:10).

Thank you for daily calling me to commune with you. I praise you for developing deep spiritual roots in me, so that I do not default to a convenient set of rules when you desire a relationship.

As I lean into your Spirit's direction, I thank you for inspiration to stand in trust—not dissolve into doubt, shy away from hard truth, or ignore your principles. In you alone, I am grateful to stand…

❋ with the confidence of **salvation** and the shield of **faith** to protect my heart and mind from the assaults of evil (Ephesians 6:16–17).

❋ with your **word** planted in my heart and applied to my life so that I am ready to accurately speak truth to others in a spirit of genuine love (James 1:22; Ephesians 4:15).

❋ with **boldness**, **compassion**, and **readiness** that replace weakness and complacency, and with eagerness to share your Good News (Acts 4:31).

Thank you for teaching me to be a peacemaker with the understanding that some will receive your truth and others will recoil.

Even so, your purposes, your plans, your authority,
and your love stand *forever*.

I gratefully anticipate new God-testimonies
as I stand on the foundation of your saving power
and kneel before your Presence.

In the name of Jesus, I pray. Amen.

Still

He says, "Be still, and know that I am God;
I will be exalted among the nations,
I will be exalted in the earth."
Psalm 46:10

He stilled the storm to a whisper; the waves of the sea were
hushed. They were glad when it grew calm, and he guided
them to their desired haven. Let them give thanks to the LORD
for his unfailing love and his wonderful deeds for mankind.
Psalm 107:29

God Who Calls Me Into Stillness,

I honor you today as the One who carries my life, counsels my mind, and breathes deep, confident calm into my soul. As I pause to reflect on you, my racing thoughts are replaced with praise, and stress begins to melt into an all-consuming knowledge that you are my true home and my resting place: my soul's serenity.

Thank you for inviting me to come away with you in stillness— to relinquish things that compete with your gentle voice. When busyness crowds your truth from my mind, it is easy to ignore or resist the guidance of your Spirit. In doing so, I invite spiritual blindness and give protection to the enemy of my soul.

But in trusting tranquility, I am able to see the ways your Spirit ministers to my spirit. And this truth dawns on my soul: your power and your peace—this indescribable wholeness—is *always offered* to me in your Presence.

Thank you for preparing a way to be still today—worshipping and listening to your Spirit. Even when the world seems out of control and oblivious to your goodness, compassion, and sovereignty, you speak hope: "For I know the plans I have for you" (Jeremiah 29:11). In the soul-searching silence my heart's secrets are laid bare, and I am grateful to cast my anxiety into your care and release my rebellion into your forgiveness (Psalm 32:5).

In the stillness, your Presence feeds my soul and fills me
with unspeakable joy and contentment.
As I gratefully acknowledge you throughout the day,
you bring new vision, new inspiration, and a new
desire to completely surrender to your purposes (Proverbs 3:6).

I am grateful to savor our time together—in sacred stillness.

In the name of Jesus, I pray and praise. Amen.

Testing

For you, God, tested us; you refined us like silver.
Psalm 66:10

When tempted, no one should say, "God is tempting me." For God cannot be tempted by evil, nor does he tempt anyone.
James 1:13

Then Jesus was led by the Spirit into the wilderness to be tempted by the devil. After fasting forty days and forty nights, he was hungry. The tempter came to him and said, "If you are the Son of God, tell these stones to become bread." Jesus answered, "It is written: Man shall not live on bread alone, but on every word that comes from the mouth of God."
Matthew 4:1–4

My Good and Steadfast God,

I am so grateful that every thought and action of yours is permeated with your love, even when I am faced with events that are extraordinarily hard and heartbreaking. When my faith, courage, or strength is tested, I am grateful to run wholeheartedly to you.

I praise you because your insight far exceeds my own grasp of events and conditions. There is no evil motive in you (Psalm 92:15). So, when you bring testing or allow trials, I thank you for leading me in paths of courage and righteousness as you strengthen my reliance on you (Genesis 15:1–6, 22:1–14).

Thank you for your work to refine my faith and character: When the earth seems to crumble beneath me, revealing the fault-lines in my thinking and heart, I thank you for drawing me close—melting and remolding me to look more like Christ (1 Peter 1:3–9).

I praise you for guiding and preserving me in persecution: Thank you for equipping me with truth and faith in the face of brutal opposition and callousness: where I see heartbreak, you see a harvest (Matthew 9:37). Thank you for instilling endurance and an undercurrent of joy when I am "counted worthy of suffering" for your sake (Acts 5:41–42). Lord Jesus, thank you for your own example of costly obedience: you bore the cross for the joy of setting me free from sin to live with you forever (Hebrews 12:2).

I am so grateful for your comfort: Thank you for wrapping me in your almighty arms when I experience pain and mourning in a world that is fallen and sinful. Thank you for the day when suffering gives way to paradise where you will wipe away every tear and even defeat death.

In the meantime, I thank you for the holiness
you are accomplishing in my life so that I may honor you
and join you in bringing light to your world.

In the name of Jesus, I pray. Amen.

Transform

And we all, who with unveiled faces contemplate the Lord's glory, are being transformed into his image with ever-increasing glory, which comes from the Lord, who is the Spirit.
2 Corinthians 3:18

I will give them an undivided heart and put a new spirit in them; I will remove from them their heart of stone and give them a heart of flesh.
Ezekiel 11:19

The law of the LORD is perfect, refreshing the soul. The statutes of the LORD are trustworthy, making wise the simple. The precepts of the LORD are right, giving joy to the heart. The commands of the LORD are radiant, giving light to the eyes.
Psalm 19:7–8

God Who Works Wonders,

You are the Gracious God who transforms me, weaving your power and your preferences into my soul. I praise you for your authority to achieve a fundamentally different way of living, so that praise and thankfulness flow naturally from my heart.

Thank you for focusing my mind not on the distress of evil in the world but on the *promise of revival*. You are willing and able to provide a way through a wasteland, living water in the desert, and change at the very core of humanity.

❋ Thank you for enabling me to stop clinging to my old ways and comprehend a radical new view of myself as a reflection of Christ.

❋ Because you are the Overcoming One, I am equipped with such potential to change the culture that it frightens the forces of evil (2 Corinthians 2:14–16; 1 John 5:4).

❋ As you build your love, joy, and peace into my heart, I become an undeniable testimony of your transforming power and a sign of hope that points others to you (Matthew 5:13–16).

Thank you for drawing my heart to you, my loving, life-changing God—becoming the center of my thinking so that my life increasingly revolves around your holiness and your will.

I praise you for inviting me to consciously draw close to you
and embrace the work of your Spirit in me—
not as an obligation but as
a grateful obsession.

In the name of Jesus, I pray. Amen.

Trust

*Let the morning bring me word of your unfailing
love, for I have put my trust in you. Show me the
way I should go, for to you I entrust my life.*
Psalm 143:8

*The LORD is my strength and my shield; my heart
trusts in him, and he helps me. My heart leaps
for joy, and with my song I praise him.*
Psalm 28:7

*Trust in the LORD with all your heart and lean not
on your own understanding; in all your ways submit
to him, and he will make your paths straight.*
Proverbs 3:5–6

My Faithful God,

I honor you today as my Everlasting Father and Unshakable
Foundation. When I trust in you with all my heart, focusing on
the truth of your Word and the stirring of your Spirit, my own
comprehension and opinions surrender to your profoundly good will.

Thank you for reminding me that *this day* was intentionally created
by you, and I am surrounded by love that is infinitely wide (Ephesians
3:18). Because you choose to walk with me, a deep river of peace runs
from your throne into my soul. We are *together*.

I honor you as the Timeless One: your vision is unlimited. You know all things before they occur, and you alone possess complete knowledge of their ultimate meaning. Thank you for guiding me through each moment in the eternal security of your Presence.

I am so grateful that all the days of my life are firmly held in your hands. You are Almighty God: my Safe Haven and my Faithful Friend. I can trust you to be perfect, wise, and watchful.

Because you live within me, I will not fall. Even when obstacles obscure my way, enemies confront me, or my own faults catch up with me, you are still God, and I am always yours.

Thank you...

- ※ for profound peace that flows not from my circumstances but from your power (Philippians 4:6–7).
- ※ for trust that surrounds and steadies me (Psalm 28:7).
- ※ for being my Provider, my Protector, and the illumination on my path (Psalm 27:1).

Thank you for being my God: my life, *my* love,
and my trustworthy Companion—forever.

In the name of Jesus, I pray. Amen.

Understanding

God Who Sees All Things,

I praise you as the only One with complete understanding: you perceive all of my life—past, present, and future—at a glance. How reassuring it is to know that you are present everywhere, wisely weighing every thought and action.

All-Knowing God, it is impossible to have real understanding without you at the core of my thinking. So, I thank you for creating a *desire to feed my mind with your scripture* (Psalm 119:11). I am so grateful to release my emotions to you and rely on your truth with the understanding that, without you, my self-focused heart and limited vision can quickly lead me to unwise choices (Jeremiah 17:9).

I am so grateful for a heightened awareness of my new identity: "I no longer live, but Christ lives in me" (Galatians 2:20). Thank you for keeping this truth at the forefront of my thoughts, so that I live and work from my position, outlook, and power in you.

Thank you for wisdom to understand the times in which I live and grace to see those around me as beloved people you are drawing to yourself. Thank you for calling me to speak in your name and promote your agenda even if you lead me to sacrifice my preferences and suffer for your sake.

I praise you for the assurance that you are working today to bring righteousness and justice. Thank you for the promise of future perfection. It is not a matter of *if* but *when* you will restore complete harmony to your cherished creation—and your timing is perfect.

As you plant understanding in my heart,
I praise you for greater faith in you and deeper love for you.
Thank you for revealing that praising you is an act of faith,
and that you, Lord, use faith to move mountains.

In the name of Jesus, I pray. Amen.

Unseen

*Though you have not seen him, you love him; and even though
you do not see him now, you believe in him and are filled
with an inexpressible and glorious joy, for you are receiving
the end result of your faith, the salvation of your souls.*
1 Peter 1:8–9

*For our light and momentary troubles are achieving for
us an eternal glory that far outweighs them all. So we fix
our eyes not on what is seen, but on what is unseen, since
what is seen is temporary, but what is unseen is eternal.*
2 Corinthians 4:17–18

God Over All,

I adore you: the invisible, incomprehensible yet knowable God.
Thank you for opening my soul to embrace what I cannot now
see: the unfathomable power of your sacrificial love and your
living Presence: "blessed are those who have not seen and yet have
believed" (John 20:29).

Thank you for establishing your home in my heart, your truth in my
mind, and your provision in your world. I praise you for wisdom
to see your hand at work—and for faith that your purposes are
underway even when they are unseen.

My Creator-Companion, thank you for watching over me with intense
interest and insight. How satisfying it is to know that you constantly

view all things and move in ways that I have not imagined—things I will only see later in heaven.

Thank you for disclosing your path gradually so that my faith deepens, and my focus remains steadily on you (2 Corinthians 5:7). Your power and insight far eclipse human capability to guide, rescue, and heal. Knowing this reality, even my most fervent, well-intentioned prayer requests are overwhelmed by assurance that you will do what is best for your honor and my ultimate good.

I praise you because you have written the end from the beginning, and today—yes, this day—you are working in ways I cannot fathom. Only you know the battles in the heavenly places fought over my soul, my faithfulness, and my joy. When I walk in the company of forces seen and unseen that seek to steal my peace and destroy my effectiveness, I thank you for wrapping me in your protective power to defend me and teach me that you are able and reliable (John 10:10).

As your purposes sweep across your world,
I thank you for inviting me *not only* to be aware of your work,
but to join you in accomplishing good. Thank you for promising
to be with me always, filling me and fueling me with your
Spirit of strength, compassion, and peace (2 Timothy 1:7).

In the name of Jesus, I pray. Amen.

Uphold

The LORD makes firm the steps
of the one who delights in him;
though he may stumble, he will not fall,
for the LORD upholds him with his hand.
Psalm 37:23–24

Because you are my help,
I sing in the shadow of your wings. I cling to you;
your right hand upholds me.
Psalm 63:7–8

God Who Watches Over Me,

I am amazed at the depth of your love and reach of your intervention. In countless circumstances, you have stepped in to secure and strengthen my soul, body, and mind.

"He reached down from on high and took hold of me."
Psalm 18:16

Lord, my Advocate and Keeper, thank you for calling me to follow your example of costly compassion: to nurture and fan into flame the smoldering faith of others and to help—rather than trample—the weak.

As I meditate on your goodness and faithfulness, my grateful heart overflows with love for you, my self-sacrificing Savior. Thank you for securing my future; I am *never* out of your sight or away from your provision. In this life and life-after-death, I am firmly, lovingly held by you.

> *"I give them eternal life, and they shall never perish;*
> *no one will snatch them out of my hand"*
> John 10:28

I praise you for upholding my righteousness—refuting the discouragement of the enemy who seeks to cast doubt or entice me to dwell on past failures. As I turn to you, acknowledging your deliverance and authority over me, the love, joy, and peace you have promised come cascading into my soul.

As I lean into you, I am grateful for the new sense of confidence and freedom your Spirit inspires knowing that nothing can separate me from your love (Romans 8:39).

> Challenges fade into gratitude as I meditate on this truth:
> I am profoundly valued, permanently loved, and
> securely upheld by you, my good and loving God.

> In the name of Jesus, I pray. Amen.

Valuable

"The kingdom of heaven is like treasure
hidden in a field. When a man found it,
he hid it again, and then in his joy
went and sold all he had
and bought that field."
Matthew 13:44

"Look at the birds of the air;
they do not sow or reap or store away in barns,
and yet your heavenly Father feeds them.
Are you not much more valuable than they?"
Matthew 6:26

God of My Life,

More than anyone or anything, I value you, my Good Shepherd and Almighty Friend. You have breathed life into my body and new life into my soul. *"How precious to me are your thoughts, God! How vast is the sum of them!"* (Psalm 139:17).

How priceless it is to know that your thoughts of me are constant—as many as the grains of sand. You are intimately acquainted with my mind. You know what I will think and say before I speak. You know every hair on my head (Psalm 139:4; Matthew 10:30).

As I begin to grasp the depth of your care, your grief at my rebellion against you, and your miraculous work to rescue me from the power of evil, I am overwhelmed by your commitment of love.

*"Greater love has no one than this: to lay
down one's life for one's friends."*
John 15:13

❋ Thank you for teaching me to value your Presence *not* simply for what you can do for me, but what you have already accomplished. Because you treasure my soul more than your very life, you chose to bring me to yourself in love and joy that exceed my hope and expectation.

❋ Thank you for valuing me too much to let difficulty or confusion rule my days. Thank you for the privilege of calling on you when my thinking is muddled, or my choices are unclear.

❋ Thank you for inspiring me to actions beyond my human ability so that your authority is revealed.

I praise you for awakening my soul to value time in your Presence so that my thoughts are intertwined with your intentions.

Lord Jesus, I gratefully celebrate your life and your will
as I remember *this day* that you are my Bread of Life
and my Living Water—my most valued treasure.

In your name, Jesus, I pray. Amen.

Victory

It was not by their sword that they won the land, nor did their arm bring them victory; it was your right hand, your arm, and the light of your face, for you loved them.
Psalm 44:3

What, then, shall we say in response to these things? If God is for us, who can be against us? He who did not spare his own Son, but gave him up for us all—how will he not also, along with him, graciously give us all things?
Romans 8:31–32

Almighty God,

I am astounded by the scope of your strength and capacity to achieve your good purposes. You are the beginning and end of everything. There is no power that can defeat you, no strategy that can outwit you, and no human mistake or wrong choice that can overthrow your plans.

No one has fully grasped the victories you win on behalf of those who love you—the overcoming power you wield in spiritual conflict, physical battles, and contests for my heart and mind. I praise you because I don't walk alone through challenges but in the *awesome force of your Spirit*—the same Spirit who moved over the waters at creation and raised Jesus from the dead (Genesis 1:2; Romans 8:11).

Thank you for walking ahead of me, having my back, and teaching me that "hopeless" situations are opportunities to lean into you or fall at your feet. The victory is always yours.

I praise you for giving me life and taking hold of my soul to rescue me from eternal disaster. Thank you for loving me steadfastly when I have reached for the darkness and rejected your path of Light— and joined humanity in decisions that cost *your life*. Thank you for choosing the crisis of the cross for us: for laying down your life and taking it up again in divine victory (1 Corinthians 15:20–26).

I praise you for your promise to ultimately defeat all sin and even death when you return to make everything right: *"Amen. Come, Lord Jesus"* (Revelation 22:20).

Thank you for helping me embrace this reality now.
As I live in your love and power, I begin to understand that
"we are more than conquerors through him who loved us."
Romans 8:37

You are able, and you are willing to win the victory
whether I see the results now or later in heaven
when we look together at the history of my life.

Thank you. In the name of Jesus, I pray. Amen.

Voice

The voice of the LORD is powerful;
the voice of the LORD is majestic.
Psalm 29:4

For the Lord himself will come down from heaven, with a
loud command, with the voice of the archangel and with
the trumpet call of God, and the dead in Christ will rise
first. After that, we who are still alive and are left will be
caught up together with them in the clouds to meet the
Lord in the air. And so we will be with the Lord forever.
1 Thessalonians 4:16–17

My Living God,

I honor you as the One who proclaims unbiased truth and deep revelation to my soul. Thank you for the promises you have spoken: to be my Constant Companion, my Wisdom, and *my home forever.* I am left speechless in the all-consuming awareness of your Presence.

Thank you for my life—this day on earth to hear your voice as you and I, my God, view your world together. "*Each new day tells more of the story, and each night reveals more and more about God's power*" (Psalm 19:2 ERV).

Thank you for revealing the spectrum of your character as your Spirit speaks to me through scripture: thundering holy judgment (1 Samuel 2:10), proclaiming mercy (Ephesians 2:4–5), gently counseling me (Matthew 11:28–29), and compassionately consoling me (2

Corinthians 1:3–4). Thank you for revealing that you know what I need before I can define or voice my heart's concerns (Matthew 6:7–8).

Lord Jesus, I praise you as my Advocate: the One who speaks on my behalf in heaven and brings assurance and encouragement to my spirit. As Satan—and the thoughts in my own mind—accuse and criticize me, your voice drowns the negative roar with the truth of your redemption. I am a righteous, welcomed, and well-loved member of your family.

Thank you for filling the meditation of my heart with your voice:

* ✻ I am chosen (John 15:16).
* ✻ I am free from condemnation (John 3:17–18).
* ✻ I am assigned a divine purpose (Acts 1:8).

I praise you for planting words of kindness in my mind and
my mouth. Thank you for your Spirit who flows through me
like living water so that your words saturate my heart,
and your voice resonates with my voice
to spread mercy and good will.

I praise and pray in the name of Jesus. Amen.

Walk

When Jesus spoke again to the people, he said, "I am
the light of the world. Whoever follows me will never
walk in darkness, but will have the light of life."
John 8:12

Blessed are those who have learned to acclaim you, who
walk in the light of your presence, LORD. They rejoice in your
name all day long; they celebrate your righteousness.
Psalm 89:15–16

God Who Walks with Me,

This is a day *you* have made, planned, and laid out before me. I do
not have to struggle to find an elusive purpose: Your will is for me
to simply *walk with you.*

I praise you today as my Breath of Life, my Faithful Friend, and my
Guide. As I intentionally lean into you, focused on your insight and
authority, it is easy to love you with all my heart, mind, and strength
(Deuteronomy 6:5).

Lord Jesus, as I walk through this season with you, I am grateful for
awareness that you have saved me *not only* from hell but *also* to *"…*
walk in the way of love, just as Christ loved us and gave himself up
for us as a fragrant offering and sacrifice to God" (Ephesians 5:2).

All-Knowing One, you see all of time at once, and you know what
lies ahead. Thank you for your Spirit of Truth to remind me of your

promises and prepare me for the future I will experience under your watchful eyes and in your almighty company (John 16:13).

I praise you for engraving your commands on my heart and reminding me that every act of obedience advances your plans. I am so grateful to stand on your strength as I follow you into the sacred work of overcoming evil that seeks to have its way in the world. Thank you for encouraging glimpses of your intervention—although your power is so great and so pervasive that I will never be able to fully comprehend it.

As I walk with you today, I thank you for carefully crafting me to reflect your likeness, so that the brilliance of your love shines through.

Thank you for preparing everything I need
for the rest of my days, so that I can say, by your power:

*"I have fought the good fight,
I have finished the race, I have kept the faith"*
(2 Timothy 4:7).

In the name of Jesus, I pray. Amen.

Way

Jesus answered, "I am the way and the truth and the life.
No one comes to the Father except through me."
John 14:6

For you know that it was not with perishable things such as
silver or gold that you were redeemed from the empty way
of life handed down to you from your ancestors, but with the
precious blood of Christ, a lamb without blemish or defect.
1 Peter 1:18–19

For the LORD watches over the way of the righteous,
but the way of the wicked leads to destruction.
Psalm 1:6

God of Grace,

Thank you for calling me to set my eyes on things above and follow your way, not aimlessly, but authentically—with an undivided heart. In loving sacrifice beyond my comprehension, you have invited me into a new way of living (Hebrews 10:19–22). "For God took the sinless Christ and poured into him our sins. Then, in exchange, he poured God's goodness into us!" (2 Corinthians 5:21 TLB).

This knowledge changes *everything* about my life. You are my God, the Holy One, the All-Knowing Savior, and you are drawing me into a future greater than myself. *Today,* you are watching over me and working in me, and I live this moment in a state of wonder—eager to see what you will do next.

Almighty God, throughout time, you have demonstrated that nothing is beyond your power to achieve your good purposes.

❈ You are the Promise Keeper. When your people were hopelessly trapped between their enemies and the Red Sea, you rolled back the waters to provide a way to safety and a new home (Isaiah 43:16).

❈ You are the Invincible One. Thank you for working to achieve miracles beyond my imagination, "making a way in the wilderness and streams in the wasteland" (Isaiah 43:19).

❈ You are the One who holds the keys of death and hell (Revelation 1:17–18). You are the resurrected Christ: the Way to experience abundant life now and the Way to future perfection (Luke 24:1–7).

As I surrender my heart, releasing everything to you,
I praise you for your powerful work to keep me on your path
and the assurance that you will deliver me into your eternal
kingdom "without fault and with great joy" (Jude 1:24).

In your name, Lord Jesus, I gratefully pray. Amen.

Word

The Word became flesh and made his dwelling among us.
We have seen his glory, the glory of the one and only Son,
who came from the Father, full of grace and truth.
John 1:14

The Son is the radiance of God's glory and the
exact representation of his being, sustaining
all things by his powerful word.
Hebrews 1:3

Your word is a lamp for my feet, a light on my path.
Psalm 119:105

God of Truth and Power,

You are not a distant, vague, or silent force but the One whose very words create, uphold, and nourish your world. By your words, you brought forth light and life, separated sky from land, made dry ground emerge from the sea, made living creatures, formed humans in your image, and called it all good (Genesis 1:1–31; Acts 17:24–28).

Almighty God, your words carry unrivaled authority. With a word, you open hearts and doors of opportunity, alter the course of history, and exchange hostility for holy reconciliation. I praise you for enacting justice and offering forgiveness. Thank you for speaking truth immersed in kindness.

Lord Jesus, I praise you as the Living Word, the One whose life on earth perfectly expressed divine holiness and compassion. You are the *"faithful and true witness"* of God's nature and activity (John 14:7–10; Revelation 3:14). Thank you for teaching me that you *are* love and that godliness is lived in loving you and other people.

Thank you for your life-giving, heart-altering words: *"Come to me, all you who are weary and burdened, and I will give you rest"* (Matthew 11:28). In your Presence, struggles cease to consume my thinking, and I am refreshed by the knowledge of your goodness and your faithfulness.

Thank you for teaching me to trust your words and build my life upon them, like constructing a house on a deep and solid foundation. Thank you for planting your truth at the core of my soul so that crises do not wash away my confidence and faith determines my responses (Luke 6:48).

I am grateful today that your words are full of life and energy.
They are not spoken lightly or without effect:
your promises, your commands, and your purposes
are mine forever—my inspiration and my delight.

Thank you. In the name of Jesus, I pray. Amen.

Worthy

Then I looked and heard the voice of many angels, numbering
thousands upon thousands, and ten thousand times ten
thousand. They encircled the throne and the living creatures
and the elders. In a loud voice they were saying: "Worthy is
the Lamb, who was slain, to receive power and wealth and
wisdom and strength and honor and glory and praise!" [7]
Revelation 5:11–12

For he has rescued us from the dominion of darkness
and brought us into the kingdom of the Son he loves, in
whom we have redemption, the forgiveness of sins.
Colossians 1:13–14

My Creator and Sustainer,

You are my enduring Truth and my life's purpose: my God in whom
I trust. *"Great is the LORD and most worthy of praise; his greatness*
no one can fathom" (Psalm 145:3).

You are the Eternally Living One: the universe exists by *your choice*.
Its inhabitants are preserved by *your design*, and its future lies in
your hands. This, alone, deserves my everlasting praise. But there's
more...

---

[7] The "Lamb" is a descriptive name of Jesus Christ who is identified as "the
Lamb of God, who takes away the sin of the world!" (John 1:29).

I praise you for mercy that is willing, enduring, and powerful. Lord Jesus, in the universal battle between good and evil, you alone were found worthy to sacrifice yourself to secure my soul: *You gave up your life to give me life.*

Thank you for your example: your undaunted compassion, patience, and perseverance. I am so grateful that no temptation or opposition could keep you from the cross for the joy of bringing me into your family (Colossians 1:22).

Thank you for reminding me that your power and determination are available to me today. You are "God with us" (Matthew 1:23). So, when you call me into difficult places, I thank you for strength to act in a way that brings honor—not shame—to your name. Knowing that people are always watching, I thank you for faith to openly declare your worth so that those around me see evidence of your goodness (Psalm 40:3).

Thank you for peace that calms and steadies me and a life-undercurrent of joy (Romans 15:13). You are worthy of my heart's adoration and my unconditional commitment.

Thank you, my powerful Provider, for equipping me with courage
to withstand evil with truth, wisdom to guard my heart,
and your word to steer my way, so that I may live a life
worthy of your calling (2 Thessalonians 1:11).

In the name of Jesus, I pray. Amen.

Yet

Yet I am always with you;
you hold me by my right hand.
You guide me with your counsel,
and afterward you will take me into glory.
Psalm 73:23–24

"Abba, Father," he said, "everything is possible for you. Take
this cup from me. Yet not what I will, but what you will."
Mark 14:36

Jesus said to her, "I am the resurrection and the life.
Whoever believes in me, though he die, yet shall he live."
John 11:25 (ESV)

My Infinite and Intimate God,

I honor you as the *"one God and Father of all, who is over all and through all and in all"* (Ephesians 4:6). You are the Overseer of the World yet attuned—even this moment—to my inner thoughts. As I consider the paradox of your character, I am in grateful awe of you.

- ※ I praise you as the Invincible Avenger and yet the tender Shepherd.
- ※ I revere you as the Great Judge and yet my wholehearted Advocate.
- ※ I praise you as the One who accomplishes justice yet extends heartfelt mercy.

I honor you today for your relentless love and your call to love *you* unconditionally. Thank you for the abundant life you unfold as I relinquish my right to myself and embrace your Presence.

Thank you for revealing that there will be storms and chaos, yet you will remain my calm and steadfast Friend, my Righteous Rescuer, and my Safe Harbor. When the enemy of my soul comes to destroy my peace, my reputation, and even my life, you offer eternal hope, abundant favor, and satisfaction—far beyond the fleeting enticements that seek to derail me from your path (John 10:9–10).

I praise you for guiding me through situations outside my understanding or beyond my control. In my weakness your power is most clearly revealed—to me and those around me (2 Corinthians 12:9; 2 Peter 1:3).

Thank you for reminding me today that
although I live *in* this world,
I am not *of* the world. Thank you for fixing my eyes on the
higher purpose: not self-preservation or my own gratification
but surrender of this day, this life, to you.

What power, what eager anticipation, and what joy I find
in walking with you today and always, my loving God.

I praise you in the name of Jesus. Amen.

Yield

*"I am the Lord; that is my name! I will not yield
my glory to another or my praise to idols."*
Isaiah 42:8

*Blessed is the man who walks not in the counsel of the wicked, nor
stands in the way of sinners, nor sits in the seat of scoffers; but
his delight is in the law of the Lord, and on his law he meditates
day and night. He is like a tree planted by streams of water
that yields its fruit in its season, and its leaf does not wither.*
Psalm 1:1–3 (ESV)

God Who Blesses and Keeps Me,

Thank you for calling me to surrender myself to you in this moment.
You are the treasure most worth having—now and into eternity. I
am filled with humility and gratitude as I recount your sacrificial
care: you are the *"compassionate and gracious God, slow to anger,
abounding in love and faithfulness"* (Exodus 34:6).

Lord Jesus, thank you for reminding me today that your gift of
salvation is free—initiated and fulfilled by you. But daily, I will face
decisions (even costly choices) that test my willingness to yield my
desires to yours.

*"Then he said to them all: 'Whoever wants to be my disciple must
deny themselves and take up their cross daily and follow me.'"*
Luke 9:23

As I immerse my thoughts in your power and goodness, yielding to you becomes a joy. I want to run to you, not rebel against you.

❋ Thank you for calling me to consciously yield my thinking to you every day, so that a foundation of God-awareness influences my attitudes and actions—and your kingdom is advanced.

❋ Thank you for motivation and faithfulness to keep my eyes on you: to withstand the tide of time constraints, life's demands, and people who clamor for first place.

❋ Thank you for wisdom to abandon or delay "good" things in favor of your best purposes including time to commune with you.

Thank you for teaching me to yield to you in prayer as Jesus prayed: *"not my will, but yours be done"* (Luke 22:42).

As you lead me through this day, I am so grateful that every
step of obedience is recorded in heaven as you produce
a harvest of righteousness around me and in me.

In the name of Jesus, I pray and praise. Amen.

Zeal

*For to us a child is born, to us a son is given, and the government
will be on his shoulders. And he will be called Wonderful
Counselor, Mighty God, Everlasting Father, Prince of Peace. Of
the greatness of his government and peace there will be no end.
He will reign on David's throne and over his kingdom, establishing
and upholding it with justice and righteousness from that time on
and forever. The zeal of the LORD Almighty will accomplish this.*
Isaiah 9:6–7

*Never be lacking in zeal, but keep your spiritual fervor, serving
the Lord. Be joyful in hope, patient in affliction, faithful in prayer.*
Romans 12:11–12

Almighty God,

I am overwhelmed by the depth of your love, the scope of your
power, and the reality of your constant Presence: *you are zealous for
me.* I honor you alone, my Designer, Life-Giver, and Redeemer: the
Sovereign God. As I walk with you this day—wrapped in your love
and inspired by your zeal—I am amazed by your promises.

- ✳ My name is written in your book of life, I am a child of God,
  and nothing can remove me from your Presence (1 John 3:1;
  Revelation 3:5).
- ✳ As I live and work on this earth, you are with me always,
  infusing my soul with love, compassion, and peace (Galatians
  5:22–23).

❋ You are bringing a new heaven and new earth where my longing for a perfect world will be fulfilled (1 Corinthians 2:9; 2 Peter 3:13).

Thank you for teaching me to address battles of the mind and heart with praise, remembering who you are and what you have done.

❋ Because you are faithful, I can take up the shield of faith to repel the attacks of evil (Ephesians 6:16).

❋ Because you are my Savior, I can face challenges with trust in your goodness (Psalm 136:1).

❋ As you fill my mind with scripture, in the power of your Spirit, *your* words can become my first thought, and my reactions can reflect your holiness (Matthew 4:4).

Thank you for awakening my heart to be zealous for things that concern you: the honor of your name and reputation (Exodus 20:7; Isaiah 42:8), the watch-care of your people (Psalm 121:7–8; 1 Peter 5:2), righteousness and justice (Psalm 11:7), and lovingkindness (Psalm 33:5).

Thank you for inspiring a life habit of praise in me. The more I honor you, the more vividly I see your love, joy, and peace radiate through my soul. And I rejoice to see the light of your face reflected in the light of my face.

In your name, Lord Jesus, I will praise and pray forever. Amen.

*Blessed are those who have learned to acclaim you, who walk in the light of your presence, L*ORD. *They rejoice in your name all day long; they celebrate your righteousness.*
Psalm 89:15-16

Reference Verses

Are you curious about a topic expressed in these prayers? The following references are provided to help you further explore these scripture-based thoughts.

Abide
Psalm 1:1–3; Psalm 16:11; Psalm 21:6; Psalm 25:5; Psalm 105:3–5; Psalm 145:8; Isaiah 26:3; John 6:44, 56–58; John 8:31; John 15:5–16; James 1:12; 1 John 2:28; Jude 1:24–25

Always
Psalm 52:9; Psalm 119:132–134; Luke 18:1–8; John 5:15–17; 1 Corinthians 13:6–7; 1 Corinthians 15:58; Philippians 1:20; Colossians 4:6; 1 Thessalonians 5:16–18; 1 Peter 3:15

Almighty
Genesis 17:1; 2 Samuel 5:3, 10; Isaiah 14:24; Isaiah 28:29; Isaiah 44:6–8; Amos 4:13; Amos 5:14; Zechariah 7:9; Revelation 1:8; Revelation 15:2–4; Revelation 19:6

Answer
Psalm 17:6; Psalm 20:6–7; Psalm 34:4–5; Psalm 91:14–15; Psalm 119:145–148; Daniel 3:17–18; Matthew 26:39; Luke 11:9; Romans 8:26–28; Romans 11:33–36

Anxiety
Psalm 13:5–6; Psalm 46:1–11; Psalm 95:6–7; Psalm 139:23–24; Proverbs 3:5–6; Proverbs 12:25; Matthew 6:25–33; Luke 8:22–25; John 10:1–4; Romans 15:13; 1 Peter 5:7

Battle
Deuteronomy 31:6; Psalm 16:7–8; Psalm 18:2; Psalm 46:1, 7; Psalm 89:8–9; Proverbs 2:6; Proverbs 18:10; Isaiah 33:6; Matthew 5:43–44; Matthew 14:29–33; Mark 13:11; Luke 6:47–49

Become
Psalm 71:5–8; Psalm 118:14, 21–23; Psalm 136:3–4; Isaiah 12:2; Matthew 18:2–5; John 12:36; Romans 6:22; 1 Corinthians 1:26–31; 1 Corinthians 2:9; Philippians 2:14–15; 1 Peter 2:4–5; Jude 1:24

Bitterness
Lamentations 3:19–26; Psalm 109:21–22; Romans 12:2, 17–21; 1 Corinthians 13:4–7; Galatians 5:22–24; Hebrews 12:14–15; James 1:19–20; James 3:13–18

Boldness
Acts 4:13, 29–30; Romans 8:32–34; 2 Corinthians 3:5–6, 12; Ephesians 3:8–12; Ephesians 6:13–19; Philippians 1:19–21; Hebrews 3:5–6; Hebrews 13:5–6; 1 John 4:16

Change
Deuteronomy 7:9; 1 Chronicles 29:11; Psalm 40:8; Psalm 77:13–14; Psalm 102:25–27; Psalm 112:6; Isaiah 40:11; Isaiah 61:4; Jeremiah 31:33; Matthew 18:2–5; Revelation 19:16

Confess
Psalm 51:10–17; Psalm 103:8–12; Psalm 119:26–27; Psalm 130:3–4; Psalm 139:23–24; Proverbs 28:13; John 1:29; 2 Timothy 2:10; Hebrews 4:12–13; 1 Peter 3:15–18

Consider
Exodus 34:6; Psalm 31:19; Psalm 33:5, 13–15; Psalm 36:5-9; Psalm 103:4; Psalm 111:4; Psalm 119:33–35; Zephaniah 3:17; John 15:9–12; Hebrews 12:1–3; 2 Peter 3:9

Decisions

Psalm 25:9; Psalm 40:8; Psalm 119:34–35, 105, 133; Psalm 139:9–10; Proverbs 3:5–6; Proverbs 16:9; Proverbs 4:11–12; Acts 2:28; Ephesians 2:10; James 1:5–8

Delight

1 Samuel 15:22; 2 Samuel 22:20; Psalm 37:1–6; Isaiah 9:6; Luke 15:20; John 10:27; John 15:9–11; Romans 8:28; Ephesians 1:4–6; Ephesians 3:20–21; 1 Timothy 6:17; 1 John 3:1

Desire

Hosea 6:6; Psalm 145:16–19; Proverbs 19:21; Isaiah 26:8; Isaiah 55:10; Mark 4:18–20; Romans 7:18, 25; Ephesians 2:1–5; 2 Thessalonians 1:11; James 4:1–3; 1 Peter 1:14–15

Devote

1 Kings 8:61; 1 Chronicles 22:19; 1 Chronicles 28:9; 2 Chronicles 16:9; Psalm 1:6; Psalm 37:5–6; Matthew 6:20–21; Mark 12:30; Acts 2:42–47; Romans 12:1–2, 10–11; Colossians 4:2

Discipline

Psalm 48:14; Proverbs 5:22–23; Proverbs 12:1; Malachi 3:2–3; 2 Corinthians 6:16; Philippians 2:12–13; Colossians 2:6–8; 1 Thessalonians 5:19–24; 2 Timothy 1:7; Hebrews 12:5–11; Revelation 3:19–20

Encourage

Psalm 10:17; Luke 12:29–32; Romans 8:31, 37; Romans 12:6–8; Romans 15:5–7; 2 Corinthians 13:11; Philippians 2:1–2; 1 Thessalonians 4:17–18; 1 Thessalonians 5:9–11; 2 Timothy 4:2

Endure

2 Chronicles 20:21–22; Psalm 100:4–5; Psalm 111:3–4; John 10:28; Romans 5:1–5; 1 Corinthians 10:13; Colossians 1:10–12; 1 Timothy 6:10–11; Titus 2:2; Hebrews 12:3

Enemies

Esther 3:5–6; Esther 4:14; Matthew 5:14–16; Luke 23:33–34; John 3:16–17; John 12:46; John 14:16–17; Romans 5:8; Romans 12:17–21; 2 Corinthians 10:3–5; Colossians 1:21–23; 1 Peter 3:18

Establish

Exodus 15:17; Psalm 9:7–9; Psalm 24:1–2; Psalm 74:16; Psalm 78:5–7; Psalm 93:1; Luke 22:19–20; Romans 16:25–27; Philippians 1:4–6; Hebrews 8:10; Hebrews 9:11–15

Faith

Psalm 92:1–2; Psalm 145:13–19; Matthew 6:30–32; Matthew 9:27–30; Matthew 14:28–33; Luke 17:5–6; Luke 22:42–43; Romans 3:22–24; 1 Peter 1:6–9

Faithful God

Psalm 33:4; Psalm 73:26; Psalm 92:1–2; Habakkuk 3:17–19; Matthew 6:30–33; Philippians 2:8; 1 Corinthians 1:8–9; Ephesians 2:4–9; Hebrews 11:23–34; Hebrews 12:2

Faithful Life

Psalm 103:11–18; Luke 1:79; Luke 4:18–21; 1 Corinthians 1:8–9; 1 Corinthians 3:10–11; Ephesians 3:20–21; Philippians 2:10–11; 1 Thessalonians 5:23–24; 2 Thessalonians 1:11; 2 Timothy 4:7–8; Revelation 1:4–6

Fear

Joshua 1:9; Psalm 27:1; Psalm 56:4; Psalm 112:1, 7; Psalm 139:16; Matthew 6:31–33; Luke 12:32; John 6:16–21; John 14:27; Romans 8:15; 2 Timothy 1:7; 1 John 4:18

Finish

Psalm 90:4; Psalm 103:19; Psalm 143:8; John 10:9–10; John 14:6; John 17:1–4; Colossians 1:25–28; 1 Thessalonians 5:23–24; 1 Timothy 1:17; 2 Timothy 4:7–8; 2 Peter 3:8–13; Revelation 21:1–6

Follow Me

Psalm 23:1–3; Luke 14:27; John 6:35; John 7:37–39; John 10:27–30; Matthew 4:18–20; Matthew 13:44; Matthew 26:39–42; Mark 8:34–38; Romans 12:1; Hebrews 12:1–2

Forgiven

Psalm 19:12; Psalm 32:1–5; Micah 7:18; Matthew 26:27–28; Mark 2:9–12; Mark 3:28–29; Luke 24:46–48; Acts 13:38–39; Colossians 1:9–14; John 14:6; 1 John 1:9–10

Forgiving Others

Psalm 25:16–20; Psalm 51:10–13; Matthew 5:23–24, 43–45; Matthew 6:12–15; Matthew 18:21–35; Luke 6:35–38; Hebrews 12:14–15; Ephesians 4:32

Generous

1 Chronicles 29:14; Psalm 145:6–9, 16; Luke 15:11–24; Romans 5:8; Romans 8:32; 2 Corinthians 9:6–11; Ephesians 1:3–10; 1 Timothy 6:18; James 1:5–6; 1 John 3:1–2

Genuine

Psalm 92:15; Isaiah 44:8; John 1:9–12; John 4:23; John 17:3; 2 Corinthians 6:3–7; Ephesians 4:22–24; Philippians 4:8–9; James 1:22–26; Revelation 4:11

Government

1 Kings 3:9–10; 1 Chronicles 29:10–12; Proverbs 8:12–16; Isaiah 9:6; Isaiah 40:22–25; Luke 20:20–26; Romans 13:1–2; Titus 3:1–8; Hebrews 10:24; Hebrews 13:17; James 1:5; 1 Peter 2:13–15

Grace

John 1:14–17; Romans 3:23; Romans 6:1–4; Romans 8:32; 2 Corinthians 6:1–2; 2 Corinthians 12:9; Colossians 4:6; 2 Thessalonians 2:16–17; 2 Timothy 1:9; Titus 2:11–14; Hebrews 2:9

Grief

Deuteronomy 31:8; Psalm 139:7–10; Isaiah 53:3–5; Mark 14:34–36; John 11:32–36; John 16:16–22; 2 Corinthians 1:3–4; Colossians 2:13–14; 1 Thessalonians 4:13; 1 Peter 1:3–6

Heart

Deuteronomy 4:9; Deuteronomy 6:5–6; Psalm 19:14; Psalm 26:2; Psalm 33:11; Psalm 43:4; Psalm 86:11; Psalm 103:11; Psalm 119:11; 2 Corinthians 4:6; Colossians 3:1; Ephesians 3:16–19

Heartache

Psalm 16:7–8; Psalm 119:28–30; Psalm 139:16–18; Matthew 11:29; John 14:27; John 16:33; Acts 28:27; Philippians 4:6–7; Colossians 3:1-3, 15; Hebrews 12:2; 1 Peter 3:18

Heaven

Psalm 73:25–26; Matthew 6:19–20; Luke 10:20; Luke 15:7; Philippians 3:20; 1 Thessalonians 4:13–18; Hebrews 1:10–12; 2 Peter 3:13; Revelation 3:12; Revelation 19:11–16; Revelation 22:1–4

Honor

1 Chronicles 16:8–11; Psalm 50:14–15; Psalm 62:7; Isaiah 57:15; Romans 11:33–36; 1 Timothy 1:17; 1 Timothy 6:13–16; Hebrews 2:6–9; Revelation 5:11–13; Revelation 7:11–12

I AM
Psalm 18:2; Psalm 36:7–9; Psalm 90:1–2; Psalm 145:3–9; Isaiah 42:7; Ephesians 1:4–10; Colossians 1:15–20; 1 Timothy 5:13–16; Jude 1:24–25; Revelation 1:17–18

Instruction
Psalm 16:7; Psalm 25:8–9; Psalm 119:105; Proverbs 9:9–10; Proverbs 13:13–14; Luke 11:1–4; 1 Corinthians 1:18–24; Ephesians 4:22–24; Colossians 2:2–4; 2 Timothy 2:25; 2 Timothy 4:2

Integrity
Leviticus 19:2; Deuteronomy 32:4; Psalm 16:7–8; Psalm 23:3; Psalm 36:5–9; Matthew 5:14–16; Ephesians 2:10; Ephesians 4:17–27; Philippians 4:6–7; Hebrews 4:12; Hebrews 12:11

Intercede
1 Kings 13:6; Psalm 106:20–23; Isaiah 53:5–6, 11–12; Isaiah 59:15–16; Romans 8:26–27, 34; 2 Thessalonians 1:11; 1 Timothy 2:1–6; 1 Peter 2:24–25

Joy
Psalm 16:5–7; Psalm 19:8; Psalm 31:7; Psalm 43:4; Psalm 51:12; Proverbs 12:20; Luke 2:8–11; Luke 6:22–23; Romans 12:12; Romans 15:13; James 1:2–4; 1 Peter 1:8–9

Justice
Lamentations 3:22; Psalm 11:4–5; Ecclesiastes 3:7–8; Romans 3:23; Romans 8:26–28; Romans 12:17–20; 2 Corinthians 10:3–5; Ephesians 1:18–21; 1 John 4:4; Revelation 15:3

Kindness
Isaiah 63:7–9; Jeremiah 9:23–24; Jeremiah 31:3; Hosea 11:4; Acts 4:8–10; Acts 14:16–17; Romans 2:4–6; 1 Corinthians 13:4; 2 Corinthians 6:3–10; Galatians 5:22–23; Ephesians 2:4–7; Ephesians 4:32

Knowing God
2 Chronicles 20:21; Matthew 6:6–8; John 10:2–4; John 14:23; Romans 8:29; Romans 15:3–4; Hebrews 10:30; James 1:5; James 4:8; 1 Peter 1:3–4; 1 John 3:1–2; 1 John 5:20

Knowledge
2 Chronicles 1:11–12; Psalm 1:1–3; Psalm 119:66; Psalm 143:8; Proverbs 3:5–6; Proverbs 21:2; Daniel 2:21–22; Romans 11:33–36; 1 Corinthians 1:5; Colossians 1:9–14; 2 Peter 1:2–3

Lament
Psalm 102:17–18; Psalm 119:169–173; Psalm 130:1–5; Psalm 142:1–2; Psalm 145:17–18; Isaiah 58:9–11; Habakkuk 3:2; Matthew 5:3–4; Romans 8:18; 2 Corinthians 4:17–18; Revelation 21:3–4

Leadership
Psalm 48:14; Matthew 5:13–16; John 10:3; John 16:13; Romans 13:1; Ephesians 1:18–23; Ephesians 4:1–2, 29; 1 Timothy 2:1–4; Hebrews 13:7, 17; 1 Peter 2:13–15, 24–25

Listen
Psalm 4:3; Psalm 5:3, 11; Psalm 10:17; Psalm 19:14; Psalm 51:8–12; Psalm 66:18–20; Psalm 139:17; Mark 9:7; John 18:37; Luke 8:16–18; John 6:35; John 7:38; Acts 4:18–20

Love
Deuteronomy 30:19–20; Psalm 11:7; Psalm 18:1–2; Psalm 103:8–11; John 1:29; John 3:16; John 10:11; John 13:34; John 15:9–11; 1 Corinthians 13:4–7; 1 John 4:8–9, 19–21

Meditate
Joshua 1:8–9; 1 Samuel 12:24; Psalm 19:8; Psalm 48:9–10; Psalm 77:10–14; Psalm 119:13–16, 58–60; Psalm 145:5; John 8:12; John 14:6; John 16:13; 1 John 4:1–6

Mercy

Psalm 28:6–7; Psalm 51:1, 10; Psalm 57:1–3; Psalm 116:1–2; Hosea 6:6; Micah 6:8; Micah 7:18; Ephesians 1:4–6; Ephesians 2:4–5; Hebrews 12:28–29; Hebrews 4:14–16

Miracles

Matthew 1:18–25; Matthew 7:9–11; Matthew 13:54–58; Luke 4:40–41; John 4:13–14; John 6:10–14; John 11:43–44; John 21:25; Acts 2:1–4, 22–24; Hebrews 2:3–4

Near

Deuteronomy 30:14; Psalm 5:12; Psalm 23:1; Psalm 32:7; Psalm 63:7–8; Psalm 119:151; Jeremiah 33:2–3; Luke 24:32; John 14:23–26; Romans 10:8–10; Ephesians 2:13; 1 John 4:10–15

New Creation

Psalm 116:5; Isaiah 61:3–4; Isaiah 64:8; Ezekiel 36:26; Matthew 5:14; Luke 22:19–20; John 8:12; Romans 6:4; Ephesians 1:18; Ephesians 4:22–24; Colossians 1:9–13; Hebrews 9:15

Open

Genesis 3:1–6, 22; Psalm 8:3–5; Psalm 119:18; Matthew 3:16; Matthew 7:7; John 10:3–4; John 17:22–23; Luke 24:45–47; Acts 26:15–18; Hebrews 10:19–23; Hebrews 13:15

Opposition

Psalm 18:2; Psalm 37:1–3; Psalm 55:16–18; Psalm 118:5–7; Psalm 124:6–8; Matthew 18:15–17; Romans 8:28, 35-37; 2 Timothy 2:24–26; Hebrews 12:14–15; 1 Peter 2:12

Overcome

Exodus 14:13–14, 29-31; Psalm 27:11–14; Psalm 54:1–4; Psalm 86:1–7; Psalm 116:1–7; Psalm 121:1–2; Zechariah 2:5; Matthew 16:18; Mark 9:17–29; Romans 8:31–39

Patience
Psalm 103:8–12; Proverbs 19:11; Joel 2:12–13; Luke 15:11–32; Romans 2:3–4; Romans 8:22–25; Romans 12:12; 1 Timothy 1:15–17; 2 Timothy 4:2; Hebrews 6:12; Hebrews 11:6

Peace
Numbers 6:24–26; Psalm 37:37; Isaiah 9:6; Malachi 2:5; Matthew 5:9; Luke 2:13–14; John 14:26–27; Romans 5:1; 1 Corinthians 1:18; Galatians 5:22–23; Colossians 3:15; I Peter 5:7

Perseverance
Isaiah 55:10–11; Luke 8:11–15; Romans 5:1–4; 1 Corinthians 9:24–27; 1 Corinthians 13:6–7; Ephesians 1:18–22; Hebrews 3:1–6; 2 Peter 1:3–8; 2 Peter 3:3–8; James 1:2–4; James 5:11

Pleasure
Psalm 16:11; Psalm 135:3; Psalm 147:10–11; Proverbs 2:6–10; Proverbs 3:13–17; Matthew 3:16–17; John 10:10; Galatians 6:8; Ephesians 5:8–10; Colossians 1:9–12; Hebrews 11:5–6

Power
2 Chronicles 32:7–8; Psalm 18:16–19; Psalm 106:68; Isaiah 40:28–31; Matthew 3:11; Matthew 4:24; Matthew 24:30–31; Acts 1:8; Romans 5:6; Ephesians 6:10–13; 1 Peter 1:3

Questions
Psalm 69:13; Psalm 91:14–16; Psalm 118:21; Mark 8:27–29; Luke 11:5–13; John 6:68; John 16:33; 1 Timothy 3:16; James 1:5; 1 Peter 3:15; 2 Peter 1:3

Quiet
Job 40:1–5; Psalm 32:1–5; Psalm 46:10; Psalm 85:8; Ecclesiastes 9:17; Habakkuk 2:19–20; Mark 1:21–27; Romans 12:18–19; 2 Corinthians 10:4–5; Philippians 2:8–16; 2 Peter 3:3–9

Raise

Matthew 28:5–9; John 5:28–29; John 6:40; John 11:21–26, 43–44; Romans 6:5–12; Romans 10:9; 1 Corinthians 15:20; 2 Corinthians 5:15; Ephesians 2:4–7, 19–22; 1 Thessalonians 4:16–17

Rebellion

Exodus 34:6–9; Psalm 107:17; Isaiah 46:8–10; Hosea 14:9; Romans 2:4–7; Romans 3:23–24; Romans 13:1–2; 1 Thessalonians 5:22–24; Hebrews 3:12–13; 2 Peter 3:9

Receive

Psalm 27:10; Matthew 7:7–11; John 20:21–22; Acts 1:8; Acts 2:36–39; Romans 8:23–25; 1 Corinthians 15:3–4; Ephesians 4:1–3; James 1:6–8; 1 Peter 4:10; Revelation 4:11

Reconcile

Genesis 45:4–7; Isaiah 53:5; Matthew 10:32–39; Romans 12:18; 1 Corinthians 1:18; 2 Corinthians 5:18–20; 2 Corinthians 13:11; Galatians 5:22–26; Colossians 1:15–20; Colossians 2:2–3

Rejoice

Leviticus 23:40–43; Deuteronomy 12:7; Psalm 5:11; Psalm 118:22–24; Psalm 119:14, 74; Habakkuk 3:17–19; Luke 2:10–11; Luke 10:17, 20; Philippians 4:8; Hebrews 12:22–24; Revelation 4:11

Remain

Psalm 27:13–14; Psalm 102:25–27; Matthew 7:24–25; John 1:29–34; John 3:36; John 8:31; John 15:10–11; Romans 13:8; 1 Corinthians 13:13; 2 Timothy 2:13; Revelation 21:1–5, 27

Remember

1 Chronicles 16:8–12; Psalm 103:17–18; Psalm 111:2–4; Psalm 143:5–8; Isaiah 46:9–10; Luke 23:32–42; 2 Corinthians 9:6–8; Ephesians 2:10; Hebrews 10:16–17

Restore

Psalm 19:7; Isaiah 9:6; Isaiah 40:29–31; John 7:38; John 15:13; Acts 3:19; Romans 12:2; Philippians 1:6; Colossians 3:1; Colossians 2:6–7; 2 Peter 1:3; 1 John 5:4–5

Return

1 Samuel 7:3; Psalm 116:7; Isaiah 55:11; Hosea 14:1–2; Malachi 3:7–16; Matthew 16:27; Luke 8:38–39; Luke 10:5–6; Luke 12:40; John 13:3; 1 Peter 2:24–25

Reveal

Deuteronomy 29:29; Job 12:22; Psalm 19:1–2; Isaiah 40:5; Isaiah 56:1; Amos 4:13; Matthew 16:15–17; John 14:16–17, 26; 1 Corinthians 2:9–14; 2 Timothy 1:9–10; 1 Peter 1:3–5

Righteous

Psalm 9:8–10; Psalm 36:6–9; Psalm 89:14; 2 Corinthians 3:18; Ephesians 4:22–24; 1 Timothy 6:9–12; James 5:16; 1 Peter 3:18; 2 Peter 3:13; 1 John 1:8–9; 1 John 2:1

Satisfy

Deuteronomy 8:10–11; Psalm 90:14; Psalm 104:27–28; Psalm 145:16–19; Isaiah 58:9–10; Matthew 14:14–21; Luke 6:20–21; John 4:10–14; Romans 8:15–17; Philippians 4:12–13

Search

1 Chronicles 28:9; Psalm 37:3–4; Psalm 63:3–8; Psalm 139:1–3, 23–24; Proverbs 2:3–5; Jeremiah 29:13; Matthew 6:31–33; Luke 15:3–10, 13–24; John 10:11–15; 1 Corinthians 2:10–11

Secure

2 Chronicles 20:17; Psalm 7:10; Psalm 16:11; Psalm 17:7; Psalm 91:11–12; Psalm 93:1–5; Psalm 140:12–13; Proverbs 10:9; Proverbs 18:10; Hebrews 12:28; 1 Peter 3:13–18

Sovereign

Psalm 51:10; Psalm 71:16; Psalm 73:28; Psalm 105:8; Psalm 109:21; Psalm 140:6–7; Isaiah 25:8; Isaiah 40:8–10; Isaiah 61:1–3, 11; Acts 4:18–31; Matthew 28:18; Revelation 19:6

Speak

Psalm 19:1–4; Psalm 50:14–15; Psalm 139:7–10; Isaiah 45:19; Isaiah 46:9–11; Isaiah 48:17–18; Luke 10:25–28; John 16:13; Romans 1:20; 1 Peter 1:3–5; Revelation 21:3–6

Stand

Psalm 1:1–3; Psalm 18:31–33; Psalm 89:2; Psalm 130:3–4; John 3:16–18; Acts 6:8–10; Romans 5:1–2; 1 Corinthians 15:1–5, 58; 1 Corinthians 16:13–14; Ephesians 6:11–17

Still

Exodus 14:10–14; Psalm 23:1–3; Psalm 37:5–8; Ecclesiastes 3:7; Isaiah 30:15, 18; Zechariah 2:13; Lamentations 3:25–26; Habakkuk 2:20; Mark 4:35–41; Acts 15:12; 1 Peter 3:3–4

Testing

Psalm 26:2–3; Psalm 139:23–24; Proverbs 17:3; Isaiah 28:16; Matthew 4:5-22; Luke 8:11–15; 1 Corinthians 13:3–7; James 1:2–4, 12–14; 1 Peter 4:12–16; 1 John 4:1–6; Revelation 21:4

Transform

Isaiah 43:18–19, 25; Romans 6:4, 11–14; Romans 7:21–25; Romans 12:1–2; Ephesians 2:1–10; Ephesians 4:22–24; Philippians 3:20–21; Colossians 3:1–10; James 4:1–8; 1 Peter 1:18–23

Trust

Numbers 20:12; Psalm 31:3–5, 14–16; Psalm 33:11–22; Psalm 46:1–3; Psalm 139:16–18; Psalm 145:13; Isaiah 26:3–4; Romans 15:13; 2 Timothy 2:11–13; Revelation 21:5–6

Understanding
Psalm 32:9; Psalm 33:13–15; Psalm 46:10; Psalm 119:10–11; Luke 2:41–47; John 17:1, 25–26; Romans 8:38–39; Ephesians 3:16–19; Philippians 4:6–7; Colossians 1:9

Unseen
Deuteronomy 29:29; Psalm 77:19–20; Matthew 6:1–6; John 1:18; John 5:37; John 6:46–47; Romans 1:20; Colossians 1:15–17; 1 Timothy 1:17; Hebrews 4:13; Hebrews 11:1–3; 1 John 4:12

Uphold
Exodus 15:2; 2 Chronicles 6:36–39; Psalm 73:23; Psalm 139:7–10; Psalm 140:12; Psalm 145:14–16; Isaiah 9:7; Isaiah 41:10; Micah 7:9; Philippians 3:7–12; Hebrews 1:1–3

Valuable
Psalm 19:9–10; Psalm 40:5; Psalm 89:15–16; Matthew 6:19–21; Matthew 12:9–13; Philippians 2:3–4; 1 Timothy 4:8; Hebrews 11:24–26; James 1:17; James 5:7–8

Victory
Genesis 1:1–2; Proverbs 21:30–31; Matthew 12:20–21; Romans 7:22–25; 1 Corinthians 2:9; 1 Corinthians 15:55–57; 2 Corinthians 10:3–5; Ephesians 1:18; 1 John 5:3–5; Revelation 22:12–13

Voice
Deuteronomy 30:19–20; Joshua 1:8–9; 1 Kings 19:11–12; Psalm 5:3; Psalm 95:6–9; Psalm 116:1–2; Isaiah 6:8; Mark 9:2–7; John 5:24; John 10:3–4; Romans 15:5–7; Hebrews 3:7–8; Revelation 3:20

Walk
Genesis 17:1; Leviticus 26:12; Deuteronomy 5:33; Deuteronomy 6:5–7; Psalm 23:4; Isaiah 40:30–31; Colossians 3:2–10; 1 John 2:6–11; 2 John 1:6; Revelation 21:1, 23–27

Way

Matthew 5:13–16; John 5:21–24; John 10:1–11; John 11:25; Acts 1:1–11; Acts 3:26; Romans 7:5–6; Romans 8:26–27; 1 Timothy 2:5; 1 John 4:14–19; Revelation 21:3–6

Word

Psalm 18:30; Psalm 33:4–6; Isaiah 40:8; Isaiah 55:10–11; Luke 1:36–37; Luke 4:31–32; Luke 21:33; John 1:1–3; John 6:63–69; Hebrews 4:12; 1 John 1:1–3

Worthy

Psalm 8:3–5; Psalm 18:3; Psalm 119:35–37; Psalm 145:13; Isaiah 25:9; Matthew 3:11; Matthew 10:37–38; Luke 12:6–7; Acts 5:29–33, 41–42; Ephesians 4:1–2; Revelation 4:11; Revelation 5:6–10

Yet

Psalm 19:1–44; Psalm 43:5; Isaiah 57:15; Habakkuk 3:17–18; Matthew 16:24–27; John 4:23–26; John 10:17; John 16:13; Romans 4:18–21; Ephesians 2:4–7; 1 John 1:5–7; 1 John 3:1

Yield

Numbers 6:24; Proverbs 3:13–14; Proverbs 19:11; Proverbs 14:24; Isaiah 48:10–11; Isaiah 55:10–11; Jeremiah 17:5–8; Matthew 6:31–33; Mark 4:1–20; Romans 6:13; James 5:7–8

Zeal

Psalm 145:17–21; Proverbs 23:17; Isaiah 42:10–13; Isaiah 59:1–4; Micah 6:8; John 2:13–17; John 5:17; Romans 10:1–4; Ephesians 2:1–9; Revelation 1:7–8; Revelation 5:9–14; Revelation 21:1–4

Printed in the United States
by Baker & Taylor Publisher Services